Passport
on a Plate

PASSPORT on a Plate

A Round-the-World Cookbook for Children

Diane Simone Vezza

illustrated by Susan Greenstein

SIMON & SCHUSTER BOOKS FOR YOUNG READERS

*This book is affectionately dedicated to my beautiful children Juliana and Alexander,
and to my husband, Jerry, my special love, who traveled with me
in search of recipes kids would enjoy.*

—D.S.V.

For Phil, Gina, Miriam, and Reya

—S.G.

ACKNOWLEDGMENTS

Special gratitude to recipe expert Margaret Happel for her editorial work on this book,
and for her encouragement, expertise, and support. Many thanks to my extraordinary editor,
Andrea Davis Pinkney. And thanks to my agent, Martha Millard, for her encouragement and guidance.
With great thanks and appreciation, too, to my family and friends who have shared
their kitchens, recipes, and heritages with me. —D.S.V.

SIMON & SCHUSTER BOOKS FOR YOUNG READERS

An imprint of Simon & Schuster Children's Publishing Division

1230 Avenue of the Americas, New York, New York 10020

Text copyright © 1997 by Diane Simone Vezza ; illustrations copyright © 1997 by Susan Greenstein

Simon & Schuster Books for Young Readers is a trademark of Simon & Schuster.

Book design by Heather Wood. The text for this book is set in Carmina Medium.

The illustrations were created by drawing with a white pencil over black gouache paint.

The illustrator then eliminated all tone with the use of a copier so that the images resemble woodcuts.

Manufactured in the United States of America.

First Edition

1   3   5   7   9   10   8   6   4   2

Library of Congress Cataloging-in-Publication Data

Vezza, Diane Simone.

The whole world cookbook / by Diane Simone Vezza. - 1st ed

p.   cm.

Summary: Describes the culinary styles of twelve regions around the world
and provides recipes for each, including Africa, the Caribbean, and China.

ISBN 978-1-4814-8812-9

1. Cookery, International—Juvenile literature. [1. Cookery, International.] I. Title.

TX725.A1V48   1997   641.59—dc21   96-50409   CIP   AC

CONTENTS

FRANCE

GERMANY

INDIA

ITALY

JAPAN

MEXICO

MIDDLE EAST

RUSSIA

VIETNAM

A NOTE TO PARENTS:

Before you and your child start cooking, read this!

To make the recipes in this book easy to use, each has been rated for its level of difficulty with a "utensil rating." The ratings are indicated with one to four utensils—a spoon, a fork, a spatula, and a knife—with all four utensils showing that a recipe is the most difficult. This means the recipe involves chopping or deep frying, and requires vigilant adult supervision and assistance. Recipes with a rating of one utensil—a spoon—can be done by a child with little adult help.

The following is a key to using the rating system most effectively:

One Utensil ♦

These recipes involve few dangerous elements. Skills include arranging, building, or shaping uncooked or cooled elements such as fruit, dough, or canned goods. Little adult supervision is required.

Two Utensils ♦

These recipes are slightly more dangerous. They may involve some or all of the following: light cutting, chopping, and dicing; baking and handling of hot dishes; use of a blender; and boiling and draining. Background supervision and assistance is suggested for these recipes.

Three Utensils ♦

These are more difficult recipes which require direct adult supervision and assistance. Potentially dangerous elements include: use of a food processor or electric mixer; stirring or turning of items that are cooking either on a stove or in the oven; delicate cutting and chopping; and use of two pans simultaneously.

Four Utensils ♦

The most difficult recipes in the book, those with a four-utensil rating, require hands-on adult interaction. In addition to the activities required for a three-utensil rating, these recipes may require high-heat cooking methods such as grilling/barbecuing, broiling, and deep-fat frying.

Note: Adult supervision is recommended when children are preparing any of these recipes, regardless of rating, and children should never be permitted to handle sharp or hot objects when an adult is not present.

AFRICA

Africa, a rich

and beautiful place with many types of people and some of the most delicious foods in the world, is a continent made up of 54 countries. Africa's land is different from region to region. The African continent has desert, grassland, rainforests, and snow-covered mountains.

Africans speak over 2,000 languages and dialects, and the people of Africa have many different backgrounds. Some are black African, some are Arab, some are of European descent. East Indian people also call Africa their home.

The food in Africa, and the way food is prepared, is as diverse as the

people. In some areas of Africa, men farm the land while women cook and take care of children. Those who live in small villages don't always use modern tools or machines. They often farm with wooden ploughs that are pulled by oxen. In some African villages, the food is prepared with the same tools that have been used for hundreds of years—tools like the mortar and pestle which grind grains and spices.

A mortar is a sturdy bowl that holds the food. The pestle is a bat-shaped stick used for grinding food.

Many villagers cook with fire, the same way their ancestors did. In large cities, people cook with stoves and ovens.

Rice, corn, squash, peas, spinach, okra, and eggplant grow abundantly in

Africa. So do pumpkins, nuts, and yams. Africans cook yams in many different ways.

A lot of Africa's food is spicy-hot. A popular African pepper is called *pilli-pilli* which is stronger than, but similar to, cayenne pepper found in the United States. Some Africans believe pepper helps the body resist infection and disease. And in some parts of Africa, there is an old belief that says a husband can tell how much his wife loves him by the amount of pepper she uses in her cooking.

An East or West African lunch or dinner can be a thick stew or soup that is eaten with a starchy food called *fufu*. *Fufu* is made by boiling cassava, yam, plantain, or rice, then pounding it with a mortar and pestle. The stew is placed on individual plates or bowls and the *fufu* or rice is served on a big plate in the center of the table so that everyone can share.

Those who are eating break off a piece of *fufu* and use it to scoop up the other foods from their plate. The *fufu* or rice helps lessen the spiciness of the main dish.

Africans snack on plantains, roasted melon seeds, sauteed almonds, and black-eyed pea balls, which they call *akara*.

Chapitis, a puffy fried bread found in East Africa, is also a popular snack. These snack foods are sold on the street in cities.

To get a taste of the African continent, try the recipes on the following pages. And don't worry—the recipes aren't spicy at all!

LOOK WHAT'S COOKING IN
AFRICA

African Fruit Salad · ∏

There are many varieties of fruits grown in Africa. In Nigeria, fruit salad is served as a first course at special occasions. If you like, you can toast the coconut by spreading it evenly on a cookie sheet. Bake at 325° F for 10 minutes, or until golden.

4 ripe papayas or mangoes, peeled, seeded and cut into bite-size pieces
2 red apples, cored and chopped
2 ripe bananas, peeled and sliced
1 16-ounce can pineapple tidbits, well-drained
1 cup fresh orange juice
1 tablespoon granulated sugar
1/2 teaspoon ground cinnamon
1/3 cup sweetened shredded coconut

In large bowl combine papayas, apples, bananas, pineapple, orange juice, sugar, and cinnamon. Toss to mix well. Cover and chill until ready to serve. To serve, sprinkle with shredded coconut.

Makes 6 servings.

Black-eyed Pea Balls ·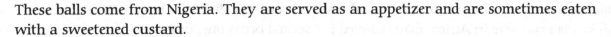

These balls come from Nigeria. They are served as an appetizer and are sometimes eaten with a sweetened custard.

> *1 cup frozen (thawed) or canned black-eyed peas,*
>   *drained and rinsed*
> *1 large egg*
> *1/2 cup chopped onion*
> *1 teaspoon salt*
> *1/4 teaspoon cayenne pepper*
> *Vegetable oil*

In medium-size bowl mash black-eyed peas with a potato masher or fork until smooth. Stir in egg, onion, salt, and cayenne pepper.

In 10-inch skillet heat 1 inch oil over medium heat to 375° F. on deep-fat thermometer. Or heat oil in electric skillet to 375° F. Drop mixture by teaspoon-fuls into hot oil. Cook 2 to 3 minutes until golden. Using slotted spoon, place on paper towels to drain.

Makes 28 balls.

Chicken Stew · ⅏

This tomato-flavored chicken stew, called *luku*, is a favorite dish in Ethiopia. Because chicken is expensive in Africa, *luku* is saved for special occasions, or guests.

3 large eggs
2 tablespoons vegetable oil
1 large onion, chopped
1 large clove garlic, crushed
1 3-pound chicken, cut up, or
1 3-pound package pre-cut chicken pieces
1 6-ounce can tomato paste
3/4 cup water
2 teaspoons paprika
1 teaspoon salt
1/2 teaspoon ground black pepper

Place eggs in medium-size saucepan; add cold water to cover by 1 inch. Over medium heat, in covered pan, bring eggs to boiling; cook 10 minutes; drain. Place pan under cold running water to cool eggs. Crack eggshells slightly; let eggs stand, covered in cold water, until ready to use.

Meanwhile, in 12-inch skillet over medium heat, heat oil; add onions; cook 5 minutes. Add garlic; cook 3 minutes longer, stirring occasionally. In drippings remaining in skillet, over medium-high heat, cook chicken pieces until well browned on all sides.

Stir in tomato paste, water, paprika, salt, and pepper. Over high heat, heat mixture to boiling, stirring to combine tomato paste. Reduce heat to low; cover and simmer 40 minutes or until chicken is tender, stirring occasionally.

Meanwhile, peel hard-cooked eggs. Using small, sharp knife, make 3 horizontal cuts on one side of each egg. Make sure the cuts are an equal distant apart, and 1/2 inch long and 1/4 inch deep. Repeat on opposite side of each egg. Add eggs to skillet; cook 5 minutes longer.

Makes 6 servings.

West African Jollof Rice •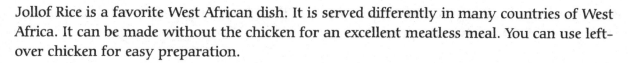

Jollof Rice is a favorite West African dish. It is served differently in many countries of West Africa. It can be made without the chicken for an excellent meatless meal. You can use left-over chicken for easy preparation.

2 tablespoons vegetable oil
1 2 1/2-pound chicken, cut up, or
1 2- to 3-pound package pre-cut chicken pieces
1 medium-size onion, diced
1 cup long-grain rice
1 13 3/4-ounce can chicken broth
1 cup water
1 6-ounce can tomato paste
1/2 teaspoon salt
1/4 teaspoon ground black pepper
1/4 teaspoon dried thyme leaves
1 9-ounce package frozen peas

In 12-inch skillet over medium-high heat, in hot oil, cook chicken pieces until well browned on all sides. Using slotted spoon, place chicken on plate. In drippings remaining in skillet, over medium heat, cook onion about 5 minutes, stirring occasionally. Add rice; cook 2 minutes, stirring constantly.

Add chicken broth, water, tomato paste, salt, pepper, thyme, and chicken pieces to skillet. Over high heat, heat to boiling; reduce heat to low. Cover and simmer 30 minutes, stirring occasionally. Stir peas into mixture; cook 10 minutes longer until peas are tender.

Makes 4 main-dish servings.

Groundnut Stew • ⫱

Peanuts are often called groundnuts, because after they flower, the plant bends down to the earth and buries its pods in the ground.

2 cups water
1 cup long-grain rice
1/2 teaspoon salt
2 tablespoons vegetable oil
1 medium-size onion, chopped
3 small sweet potatoes, peeled and cut
   crosswise into 1/2-inch thick slices
3 cups shredded green cabbage
1 13 3/4-ounce can chicken broth
1/2 cup crunchy peanut butter
3 bananas, peeled and thinly sliced
1 tablespoon chopped parsley
1/4 cup chopped unsalted peanuts

In 2-quart saucepan over high heat, heat water, rice, and salt to boiling. Reduce heat to low; cover and simmer 20 minutes until rice is tender.

Meanwhile, in 12-inch skillet over medium heat heat oil; add onion; cook 5 minutes; add sweet potatoes and cabbage. Cook 10 minutes longer, stirring occasionally. Stir in chicken broth, peanut butter, bananas, and chopped parsley; heat to boiling. Reduce heat to low; simmer, uncovered, 5 minutes until thickened. Serve mixture over rice. Sprinkle with chopped peanuts.

Makes 6 servings.

Kale and Potatoes ·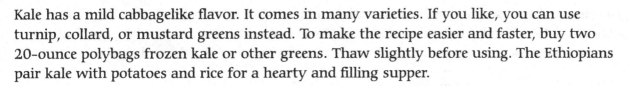

Kale has a mild cabbagelike flavor. It comes in many varieties. If you like, you can use turnip, collard, or mustard greens instead. To make the recipe easier and faster, buy two 20-ounce polybags frozen kale or other greens. Thaw slightly before using. The Ethiopians pair kale with potatoes and rice for a hearty and filling supper.

> *1 cup brown rice, see note*
> *3 tablespoons vegetable oil*
> *2 large all-purpose potatoes, cut into 1-inch chunks*
> *1 medium-size onion, chopped*
> *1 garlic clove, crushed*
> *6 cups coarsely chopped kale*
> *1 cup canned chicken broth*
> *1/2 teaspoon salt*
> *1/4 teaspoon ground black pepper*

Prepare rice as label directs. Meanwhile in 5-quart saucepan over medium-high heat, in hot oil, cook potato chunks until lightly browned on all sides, about 5 minutes. Reduce heat to medium. Add onion and garlic; cook 5 minutes longer, stirring occasionally.

Add chopped kale, chicken broth, salt, and pepper. Over high heat, heat to boiling. Reduce heat to low; cover and simmer 15 minutes until potatoes are tender, stirring occasionally. Serve over a large spoonful of brown rice.

Makes 4 servings.

Note: Brown rice takes 35 minutes to cook, so look at the package directions and begin to make it before starting the potatoes. If you buy "instant" brown rice, it will cook in just 10 minutes.

Fufu •

Fufu is an African staple that is eaten with hearty soups and stews. It tastes like a mix between potatoes and bread without a crust. And because it is fun to eat with your fingers, you can break open a warm *fufu* ball, use it to scoop up other foods, and then eat it.

2 1/2 cups water
2 cups buttermilk baking mix, such as Bisquick
2 cups instant potato flakes
1 tablespoon butter or margarine
1/4 teaspoon salt

In 2-quart saucepan over high heat, heat water to boiling. Stir in buttermilk baking mix, instant potato flakes, butter, and salt. Reduce heat to low. With wooden spoon, stir mixture constantly 10 minutes until mixture becomes very thick and hard to stir. Take care, the mixture will be very hot.

Wet a medium-size bowl. Drop 1/2 cupful of fufu mixture into bowl; shake bowl until the mixture forms a smooth ball. Repeat with remaining mixture. Serve while warm.

Makes nine 2-inch balls.

Kenyan Crunchy Bananas •

Bananas are high in potassium and vitamin C. Africans use many different types of bananas. A favorite type is the plantain which is very large and used in cooking.

1 tablespoon butter or margarine
1 tablespoon firmly packed brown sugar
1/4 teaspoon ground cinnamon
2 large bananas, medium-ripe
l/4 cup chopped unsalted peanuts

Preheat oven to 375° F. In small saucepan over low heat, melt butter; stir in brown sugar and cinnamon until well blended.

Grease 9 x 9-inch baking pan. Peel bananas; cut each banana lengthwise in half. Place cut-side down in baking pan. Brush with some brown-sugar mixture; sprinkle with chopped peanuts. Bake 20 minutes, or until bananas are lightly browned. Serve warm.

Makes 2 servings.

Little Yam Cakes ⋅ 🍴

Yams in Africa are starchier and more fibrous than the yams we have in the United States, but these little cakes are just as good when made with American yams or sweet potatoes found in a can.

3/4 cup butter or margarine, softened
3/4 cup granulated sugar
1/2 cup firmly packed brown sugar
2 large eggs
1 16-ounce can yams or sweet potatoes drained
   and mashed smooth with fork
1 teaspoon vanilla extract
1 1/2 cups all-purpose flour
1 teaspoon baking soda
1 teaspoon ground cinnamon
1 teaspoon ground nutmeg
1/2 cup chopped unsalted peanuts
Confectioners' sugar

Preheat oven to 350° F. Grease twelve 2 1/2-inch muffin pans. In large bowl with electric mixer at medium speed, beat butter, granulated sugar, and brown sugar until creamy. Add eggs, yams, and vanilla; beat until smooth. Combine flour, baking soda, cinnamon, and nutmeg; add to egg mixture. Beat 2 minutes until well blended, scraping bowl occasionally. Stir in peanuts.

Spoon batter into muffin pans. Bake 30 minutes, or until toothpick inserted in center comes out clean. Cool in pans on wire rack; remove muffins from pans. To serve, lightly sprinkle with confectioners' sugar.

Makes 12 cakes.

THE CARIBBEAN

In 1492

Christopher Columbus sighted San Salvador, an island of the Bahamas in the Caribbean. On his voyages he also went to Puerto Rico, Cuba, Jamaica, Trinidad, and Hispaniola. The Caribbean, also known as the West Indies, is a region of about one hundred islands, scattered throughout the Caribbean and western Atlantic oceans.

Chili peppers are a very popular ingredient in Caribbean cooking. Some of the world's hottest sauces are made with chili peppers and come from the islands in the Caribbean. Other favorite ingredients of Caribbean kitchens are curry, pineapple, coconut milk, and bananas.

Caribbean cooking is a blend of cultures, flavors, textures, and colors. The first settlers of the Caribbean islands were the Carib and Arawak Indians. The Arawak Indians were fishermen and farmers who grew sweet potatoes, corn, and cassava—a very large tapered, cylindrical vegetable, with a thick bark-like skin and white flesh. They seasoned their food with chili peppers and spices. After that, over a period of centuries, Spanish, Dutch, French, British, Portuguese, Danish, East Indian, and Chinese settlers came to colonize the islands bringing their foods and ways of cooking with them.

Those from India brought curry

powder. The Chinese brought Asian spices, vegetables, pickles, and chili pastes.

In the 18th and 19th centuries African people were brought to the Caribbean, and enslaved. Many believe Africans have had the greatest influence on Caribbean cooking. Africans brought okra and peas to the islands. They planted crops of these foods to make themselves feel at home.

In the early 19th century, slavery was done away with in the Caribbean, but the African flavors brought to Caribbean foods have remained.

There are many types of people and many languages spoken in the Caribbean. But each island has its own taste. For example, the cooking in the Dominican Republic and Puerto Rico uses Spanish flavors and ingredients such as olives, olive oil, garlic, and vinegar.

The people who live on the islands of Martinique and Guadeloupe use many French cooking ingredients such as French jams, fresh herbs, creamy sauces, and preserved fruits.

On the island of Curaçao, which has a strong Dutch influence, Edam cheese from the Netherlands is popular.

The island of Jamaica has a large British influence. On Jamaica, people cook with ginger beer, chutney, and curry. Jerk chicken and jerk pork are also very popular Jamaican delights. Jerk cooking originated with the Arawak Indians. They seasoned their pork and smoked it—or "jerked" the meat until it was dry and would preserve well in the tropical humidity. Today jerk cooking is still very popular.

Want to fly away to a sunny Caribbean island? Let your taste buds make the flight. Recipes for Caribbean treats are as close as the next page.

LOOK WHAT'S COOKING IN
THE
CARIBBEAN

Callaloo Soup · 🍴

Callaloo is a popular leafy green vegetable found in the Caribbean. It is like spinach or kale. Most every Caribbean island has a recipe for *callaloo* soup, and they are all different.

5 slices bacon, diced
1 medium-size onion, diced
6 cups coarsely chopped fresh spinach or kale, or
   2 20-ounce polybags frozen spinach or kale
3 cups canned chicken broth
1 6-ounce can cooked, shelled crabmeat, drained and flaked

In 5-quart saucepan over medium heat, cook diced bacon until tender-crisp, about 5 minutes, stirring occasionally. Using slotted spoon, place bacon on plate.

To drippings remaining in skillet, cook onion until tender, about 5 minutes. Add chopped spinach, chicken broth, and cooked bacon. Over high heat, heat to boiling. Reduce heat to low; cover and simmer 20 minutes.

Let mixture cool slightly. In food processor or blender, puree mixture in batches until smooth. Stir in crabmeat. Reheat soup if it is too cool.

Makes 6 servings.

Jerk Chicken ⋅

Jerked meats are Jamaica's most famous dishes. The Jamaicans make tiny holes in the meat with the tip of a knife and rub seasoning in the holes. This recipe can also be made with pork chops.

3 tablespoons firmly packed light brown sugar
3 tablespoons soy sauce
1 tablespoon fresh orange juice
1/2 teaspoon salt
1/2 teaspoon dried thyme leaves, crushed
1/4 teaspoon ground allspice
1 pound boneless, skinless chicken breasts

In large bowl combine brown sugar, soy sauce, orange juice, salt, thyme, and allspice. Lightly prick both sides of chicken breasts with tip of sharp knife or tines of fork. Add chicken to mixture; turn to coat on both sides. Cover and marinate at least 1 hour, turning occasionally.

Preheat broiler or grill. Place chicken breasts on rack in broiler pan or on grill. Cook, 4 inches from heat source, 5 to 10 minutes, turning once until chicken is cooked through.

Makes 4 main-dish servings.

Oven-Fried Yams · 🍴

Yams are a tropical root vegetable, often confused with sweet potatoes. Yams belong to a different family than sweet potatoes. Not as perfectly shaped as sweet potatoes, yams range in color from white, to yellow, to red and brown. They grow so big that they are often sold in chunks in Caribbean and Hispanic markets.

> *2 large yams, about 2 pounds, see note*
> *3 tablespoons vegetable oil*
> *3/4 teaspoon salt*
> *1/4 teaspoon ground black pepper*

Preheat oven to 425° F. Peel yams; cut into sticks, 1/2 inch thick and 3 to 4 inches long. Grease large roasting pan. In pan toss yam "sticks" with oil, salt and pepper. Spread out in one layer. Bake 30 minutes or until yams are tender, stirring occasionally.

Makes 4 servings.

Note: Sweet potatoes or Idaho baking potatoes may be used, if preferred. Sweet potatoes cook in 15 to 20 minutes.

Calypso Coconut Chicken •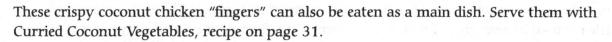

These crispy coconut chicken "fingers" can also be eaten as a main dish. Serve them with Curried Coconut Vegetables, recipe on page 31.

1 pound package boneless, skinless chicken breast halves
1/2 cup all-purpose flour
1 teaspoon baking soda
1 teaspoon salt
1 teaspoon paprika
1/4 to 1/2 teaspoon cayenne pepper, depending on taste
1/2 cup water
1 1/2 cups unsweetened shredded coconut
Vegetable oil for frying (optional)

Cut chicken breasts into 1-inch crosswise strips. In medium-size bowl combine flour, baking soda, salt, paprika, and cayenne pepper; stir in water until well blended.

Place coconut in plate or bowl. Dip a chicken piece into flour mixture; then roll the chicken in the coconut until evenly coated. Place on a plate; repeat with remaining chicken pieces, batter, and coconut.

Preheat oven to 400° F. Lightly grease large baking pan. Arrange chicken strips evenly in pan. Bake 5 to 10 minutes or until tender when pierced with a fork. Serve warm.

Makes about 24 chicken pieces, 6 appetizer servings,
or 4 main-dish servings.

Note: A more traditional Caribbean way to cook this chicken is to fry it. In deep 12-inch skillet, heat 1 inch oil to 375° F. on deep fat thermometer. Or heat oil in electric skillet set at 375° F. Carefully add chicken strips to hot oil; cook about 2 minutes, turning occasionally, until coconut is golden and chicken is tender. Remove to paper towels to drain. Serve warm. If you choose to prepare the chicken by this method, the utensil rating becomes a 4.

Jamaican Beef Turnovers •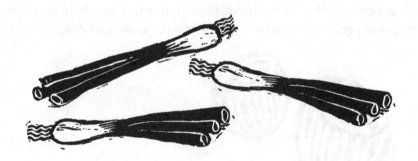

These delicious turnovers are also known as "patties" in Jamaica. The East Indians and Africans used leftover meat for their turnovers. They ground it up with some seasoning and wrapped it in a pastry crust. In Caribbean islands influenced by the British, turnovers are often called "pasties"—pronounced "pahsties."

1 pound package ground beef or turkey
2 large scallions, sliced
2 garlic cloves, crushed, or 1 teaspoon minced garlic
1 teaspoon salt
1 teaspoon paprika
1 teaspoon dried thyme leaves
3 tablespoons chili sauce
1 tablespoon Caribbean-style or other spicy brown steak sauce, optional
1 10.8-ounce container large flaky refrigerator biscuits (5 biscuits),
*   such as Pillsbury Grands*
1 large egg, lightly beaten

In 10-inch skillet over medium-high heat, cook ground beef about 5 minutes. Add scallions, garlic, salt, paprika, and thyme; cook 5 minutes longer or until beef is browned, stirring occasionally. Stir in chili sauce and steak sauce.

Preheat oven to 350° F. Grease large cookie sheet. On lightly floured surface with floured rolling pin, roll each biscuit into a 6-inch round circle. Place 1/5 of beef mixture on a biscuit round. Brush edge of pastry with beaten egg. Fold dough round in half; press edges together with end of fork to seal. Place on cookie sheet; brush turnover with egg. Repeat with remaining beef mixture, pastry and egg. Bake 18 to 20 minutes until golden.

Makes 5 turnovers.

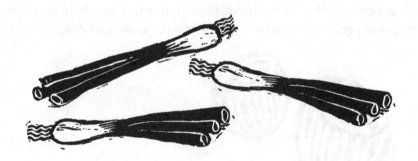

Curried Coconut Vegetables ⋅ 🍴

Coconut milk can be found in cans in the supermarket. If you can't find it, you can substitute 1/2 cup milk mixed with 1/4 teaspoon coconut extract.

2 cups water
1 cup long-grain rice
1 teaspoon salt
3 medium-size carrots, peeled and sliced
2 cups green beans, cut into 2-inch pieces
1 cup canned vegetable broth
1 tablespoon curry powder
1 large yellow summer squash, cut into bite-size pieces
1 cup frozen peas, from 9-ounce package
1/2 cup coconut milk
1/2 cup unsweetened shredded coconut
1 tablespoon cornstarch
1/4 cup water

In 2-quart saucepan over high heat, heat water, rice, and 1/2 teaspoon salt to boiling. Reduce heat to low; cover and simmer 20 minutes until rice is tender.

Meanwhile, in 3-quart saucepan over high heat, heat carrots, green beans, vegetable broth, curry powder, and remaining 1/2 teaspoon salt to boiling. Reduce heat to low; simmer uncovered 5 minutes. Add squash, peas, coconut milk, and shredded coconut to saucepan. Over high heat, heat to boiling. Reduce heat to low; simmer uncovered 5 minutes or until vegetables are tender.

In small cup, stir cornstarch and water. Stir into simmering vegetables; cook 2 minutes longer or until mixture has thickened. Serve over rice.

Makes 6 servings.

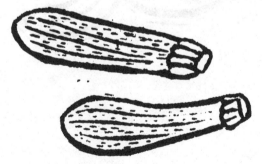

Island Banana Fritters ♦ 🍴

Bananas were one of the first plants to be grown in the Caribbean. They required little work and grew throughout the year. The Caribbean has many varieties of bananas to choose from. Bananas are high in carbohydrates, vitamins, and minerals. These fritters can be topped with vanilla ice cream if you like.

> *2 medium-size ripe bananas, peeled*
> *1 large egg*
> *1/4 cup all-purpose flour*
> *2 tablespoons firmly packed light brown sugar*
> *1/4 teaspoon ground cinnamon*
> *Vegetable oil for frying*
> *Confectioners' sugar*

In medium-size bowl mash bananas; stir in egg, flour, brown sugar, and cinnamon until mixture is well blended.

In 10-inch skillet or deep-fryer, over medium heat, heat 1 inch vegetable oil to 400° F. on deep-fat thermometer. Or heat oil in electric skillet set at 400° F. Carefully drop banana batter, one tablespoon at a time, into hot oil. Add 3 more separate tablespoonfuls of batter, so there is a batch of 4 fritters. Cook fritters about 3 minutes until golden. Using slotted spoon, place fritters on paper towels to drain. Repeat twice more with remaining batter. Sprinkle fritters with confectioners' sugar.

Makes 12 fritters.

Caribbean-Style Pineapple Snow •

If you like, you can substitute chopped fresh mango or papaya for the pineapple in this recipe. Or you can use 1 cup canned fruit cocktail, drained or 1 cup sliced canned peaches, drained and chopped.

> *1 pint vanilla ice cream (2 cups)*
> *1 cup chopped fresh pineapple or*
> *1 8-ounce can crushed pineapple, drained*
> *2 tablespoons sweetened shredded coconut, toasted if desired, see note*

Soften ice cream to room temperature, about 20 minutes. In medium-size bowl stir ice cream with pineapple until well blended. Serve immediately. Sprinkle with coconut. Or, freeze to serve later. Soften mixture slightly just before serving.

Makes 4 servings.

Note: To toast coconut, spread it evenly on a baking sheet. Bake at 325° F. for 10 minutes until golden.

Island Fruit Smoothies •

Many types of blended fruit drinks are served in the Caribbean. You can use fresh, hulled strawberries if you like with a few ice cubes.

> *2 cups frozen whole strawberries, slightly thawed, one 16-ounce polybag*
> *1 medium-size ripe banana*
> *1/2 cup fresh or canned pineapple juice*

Place strawberries, banana and pineapple juice in blender or food processor. Blend on low speed until drink is smooth. Makes two 1-cup servings.

CHINA

In China

another way to say hello is "Have you eaten?" The Chinese love and appreciate their food.

China has many extremes of geography and climate. Because of this, cooking varies from place to place. To better understand the many differences in Chinese food, it helps to think of China as being divided into four areas: North, South, East, and West. Each area boasts its own cooking style.

The North has a cool climate. Wheat is the main crop. Noodles,

steamed bread and buns, which are all made with wheat flour, are eaten in

northern China. Peking is one of northern China's largest cities. Peking duck, which was served to royalty back in ancient China, is still a popular dish for banquets.

Canton is the principal province of South China. It is also the name of the biggest city. The climate is generally warm, and there are heavy rainfalls and humidity in this region. Rice is the most common food. It is harvested twice a year, and eaten for lunch and dinner. The province of Canton is known as "the rice bowl of China."

Canton is also famous for its *dim sum*—a phrase which means "touch the heart." The phrase, *dim sum*, is also the name given to a variety of small, delicious snacks such as hot appetizers of pastry stuffed with a mixture of pork, beef, or seafood. *Dim sum* can also be

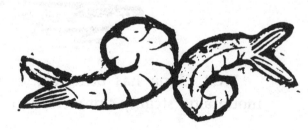

25 ❖

made up of soups, dumplings, breads, cakes, and noodles. Crispy wontons (page 38) is a popular *dim sum* recipe.

Eastern China is known as "the land of fish and rice" and "heaven on earth." The climate of Eastern China is mild. This part of the country has rainy summers and cool winters, giving it a year- round growing season. Shanghai is Eastern China's biggest city and greatest port. This area has some of the most fertile land in China, which produces many fruits and vegetables. Because of this, vegetarian meals are popular. The region has a long coastline, so fish and shellfish are abundant.

West China has beautiful, humid mountains, steamy summers, and mild winters. It is called "the land of abundance."

Szechuan, a province of Western China, is the home of many bamboo groves. Because they grow so abundantly, tender bamboo shoots are favorite food of many Szechanese people. Panda bears come from Szechuan. They eat bamboo shoots too.

Throughout China, everyone eats with chopsticks. Chinese people call chopsticks "quick brothers." Because they are used to cook with, as well as to eat, they can be made of bamboo, wood, or plastic, as well as ivory, silver, or gold. Chinese chopsticks have blunt ends. (Japanese chopsticks are pointed.)

Most Chinese restaurants in the United States provide chopsticks, and have instructions on how to use them. Or you can buy your own pair of chopsticks at Chinese specialty stores or markets. Some of the recipes that appear on the following pages are great for eating with chopsticks.

LOOK WHAT'S COOKING IN
CHINA

Crispy Wontons ·

You can make and fold these dumplings ahead of time; cover with plastic wrap, and keep in the refrigerator until you are ready to fry them. Do not make ahead more than 24 hours.

1 tablespoon peanut or vegetable oil
1/2 pound ground pork
1/2 pound shrimp, cleaned and chopped, or
*   1 8-ounce can shrimp, drained and chopped*
1 tablespoon finely chopped fresh ginger
1 garlic clove, crushed, or 1/2 teaspoon garlic powder
1 cup chopped watercress or spinach
1 tablespoon soy sauce
1 12-ounce package wonton wrappers, see note
1 egg white
Peanut or vegetable oil for frying

In 12-inch skillet over medium-high heat, in hot oil, cook ground pork, shrimp, ginger, and garlic until pork is lightly browned, stirring to break up any large pieces of pork. Take skillet off heat; stir in watercress and soy sauce until well mixed.

To fill wontons: Spoon 1 heaping teaspoonful pork mixture onto center of one wonton wrapper. With a small brush, brush edges of wrapper with egg white. Fold wrapper in half to make a triangle. Bring corners together; overlap corners, brushing with egg white; press to seal. Place on large tray. Repeat with remaining wontons and filling.

In a 3-quart saucepan, heat 2 inches peanut oil over medium heat to 350° F. Use a deep-fat thermometer to measure correct temperature. With slotted spoon, carefully add some wontons to hot oil. Cook wontons about 1 minute or until golden brown, carefully turning wontons with slotted spoon. Still using slotted spoon, place wontons on paper towels to drain. Repeat with remaining wontons.

Makes about 50 wontons.

Note: Wonton wrappers are found in the produce section of your supermarket.

Noodles and Peanut Sauce ⋅

For centuries in China, wheat flour noodles and dumplings were only eaten by those who were unable to afford rice. Today, wheat noodles are very popular, and used to make this Cantonese-style dish. You can substitute Chinese sesame paste, found in Asian grocery stores, for the peanut butter if you like a sesame taste.

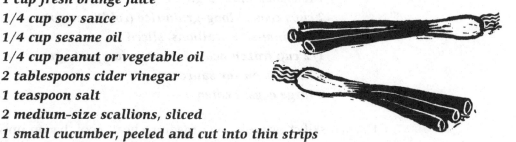

1 16-ounce box spaghetti
1 cup chunky peanut butter
1 cup fresh orange juice
1/4 cup soy sauce
1/4 cup sesame oil
1/4 cup peanut or vegetable oil
2 tablespoons cider vinegar
1 teaspoon salt
2 medium-size scallions, sliced
1 small cucumber, peeled and cut into thin strips

Cook spaghetti in boiling salted water 5 to 10 minutes until just tender. Drain. Pat dry with paper towels.

Meanwhile, in a large bowl stir peanut butter, orange juice, soy sauce, sesame oil, peanut oil, cider vinegar, salt, and scallions until well mixed. Add spaghetti; toss to mix well.

Serve warm, or cover and refrigerate to chill and serve later. Just before serving, toss with additional orange juice, if necessary. Garnish with cucumber strips.

Makes 6 servings.

Chinese Fried Rice ·

In China, fried rice is eaten as an afternoon snack rather than part of a meal. This recipe is a great way to use up cold leftover rice. It is best to start with cold rice.

2 slices bacon, diced
2 tablespoons peanut or vegetable oil
1/2 inch piece of fresh ginger, peeled and sliced, or
  1 teaspoon powdered ginger
1 teaspoon minced garlic
2 cups cooked long-grain rice (cold), see note
2 medium-size scallions, sliced
1/2 cup frozen peas, from 9-ounce package
1 tablespoon soy sauce
2 large eggs, beaten

In 12-inch skillet or wok, over medium heat, cook bacon until browned and crisp, stirring occasionally. Using slotted spoon, place bacon on paper towels to drain. In hot oil, cook ginger and garlic about 2 minutes.

Add rice to skillet; cook, stirring constantly about 5 minutes; add scallions, peas, and soy sauce. Cook 5 minutes longer, stirring occasionally until rice is lightly browned.

Make a well in center of rice; add beaten eggs. Cook over medium heat, stirring until eggs are like small peas. Stir into the rest of rice mixture.

Makes 4 side-dish servings.

Note: If you have to make the rice first, allow plenty of time so it can become completely cold before you fry it. You will need to cook 3/4 cup raw long-grain rice according to package directions.

Sesame Broccoli •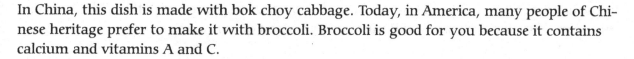

In China, this dish is made with bok choy cabbage. Today, in America, many people of Chinese heritage prefer to make it with broccoli. Broccoli is good for you because it contains calcium and vitamins A and C.

> *1 tablespoon sesame seeds*
> *1 bunch broccoli or bok choy cabbage, about 2 pounds*
> *3 tablespoons peanut or vegetable oil*
> *1/2 teaspoon salt*
> *1/2 teaspoon granulated sugar*
> *1/3 cup water*
> *2 teaspoons sesame oil*

In small nonstick saucepan over low heat, cook sesame seeds 3 to 4 minutes, shaking pan constantly until sesame seeds are lightly toasted and golden or, toast sesame seeds in toaster oven. Set aside.

Cut broccoli into 2 inch by 1/2 inch pieces. In large saucepan over high heat, in hot oil, cook broccoli pieces about 2 minutes until coated with oil, stirring constantly.

Add salt, sugar, and water; reduce the heat to medium. Cover and cook 3 minutes, or until water has evaporated. Uncover saucepan and cook 4 minutes longer, stirring occasionally. Stir in sesame oil and toasted sesame seeds.

Makes 4 side-dish servings.

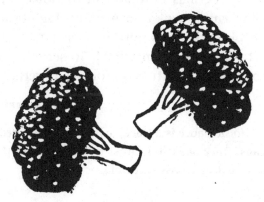

Mu Shu Pork ·

In the United States, unlike in China, thin soft pancakes are served with this dish. To make this recipe easy, we use packaged flour tortillas instead of pancakes.

3/4 pound pork tenderloin
1 tablespoon soy sauce
3 tablespoons peanut oil
2 cups shredded Chinese cabbage or Napa cabbage
2 medium-size scallions, sliced
1 cup fresh bean sprouts
1 cup sliced mushrooms
2 large eggs, lightly beaten
8 6-inch flour tortillas, from 12-ounce package
Hoisin sauce, see note

Cut pork into thin strips, about 2 x l/4 inches. Place in small bowl; toss with soy sauce. Set aside.

In wok or 12-inch skillet over medium heat in 2 tablespoons peanut oil, cook cabbage 5 minutes. Add scallions, bean sprouts, and mushrooms; cook 5 minutes longer or until vegetables are tender. Using slotted spoon, place mixture in large bowl. In drippings remaining in wok over medium heat, cook eggs, stirring constantly until eggs are set but not runny. Place in bowl with vegetables.

Wrap tortillas in foil. Heat tortillas in 350° F. oven, about 10 minutes or until warm. In wok over medium-high heat, in remaining 1 tablespoon peanut oil, cook pork strips until well browned, about 5 minutes. Place in bowl with vegetables; toss to mix well. To serve, spread some hoisin sauce on tortilla; spoon mu shu mixture on tortilla. Carefully fold 3 sides to enclose mixture.

Makes 4 servings.

Note: Hoisin sauce is a thick, sweet and spicy, reddish-brown sauce. It is found in bottles or cans. Once opened, it must be refrigerated. If you buy hoisin sauce in a can, be sure you store it in a glass jar or plastic container.

Chinese Spareribs with Plum Sauce ·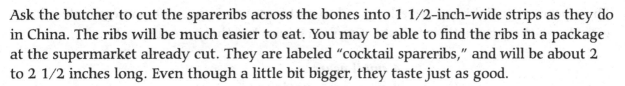

Ask the butcher to cut the spareribs across the bones into 1 1/2-inch-wide strips as they do in China. The ribs will be much easier to eat. You may be able to find the ribs in a package at the supermarket already cut. They are labeled "cocktail spareribs," and will be about 2 to 2 1/2 inches long. Even though a little bit bigger, they taste just as good.

2 pounds pork spareribs
3/4 cup Oriental plum sauce, see note
2 large scallions

Cut pork spareribs lengthwise between each bone. Place ribs in large saucepan with enough water to cover. Over high heat, heat to boiling. Reduce heat to low; cover and simmer 45 minutes or until ribs are tender. Drain well.

Heat broiler or barbecue grill. Place ribs on rack. Cook ribs, 4 inches from heat source, 10 minutes, turning once. Brush ribs with plum sauce; cook ribs turning frequently until glazed, about 5 minutes, brushing with additional sauce.

To serve, place ribs on platter. Cut scallions into 3-inch-long pieces; garnish platter with scallions.

Makes 4 servings.

Note: Oriental plum sauce can be found in a jar in the international section of most supermarkets.

Blushing Pears ⋅

These pears are a light and refreshing end to a Chinese meal. In China pomegranate juice would give these pears their "blush." Cranberry juice has the same rosy color.

> **4 small pears**
> **2 cups cranberry juice**
> **1/4 cup honey**
> **1 cinnamon stick**
> **1 whole clove**
> **1/4 teaspoon ground ginger**

Peel pears, leaving stems on. Cut a small slice off bottom of each pear so that pears stand up straight. In medium-size saucepan, combine cranberry juice, honey, cinnamon stick, clove, and ginger. Add pears, making sure that pears are completely covered with liquid. Over high heat, heat to boiling. Reduce heat to low; simmer, uncovered, 30 minutes or until pears are tender.

Using slotted spoon, carefully drain pears from liquid and place in shallow bowl (pears should be standing up). Continue simmering liquid about 15 minutes until slightly thick and syrupy. Let liquid cool to warm before spooning over pears. Serve warm, or refrigerate to serve cold later.

Makes 4 dessert servings.

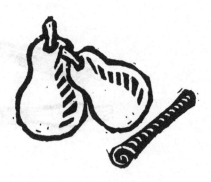

Chinese Fortune Cookies ⋄

Fortune cookies were an American invention, and were introduced to China by Chinese-Americans. This is a great project to do when you have lots of time, and all your family can help you.

1/2 cup granulated sugar
2 large egg whites
1/4 cup all-purpose flour
1/4 cup butter or margarine, melted
1/2 teaspoon almond extract

Prepare Fortunes: Cut 12 small slips of paper about 2 inches by 1/2 inches. On each paper write a fortune or saying.

Preheat the oven to 350° F. Grease large baking sheet. In large bowl stir sugar and egg whites until sugar is totally dissolved. Add flour, melted butter, and almond extract. With an electric mixer at high speed, beat until smooth.

Drop 1 heaping teaspoonful of batter onto prepared cookie sheet, about 2 inches apart. You will only have 3 or 4 cookies on each sheet, because they will spread. Bake 5 minutes or until edges are browned. Carefully remove the cookies from the cookie sheet. While cookies are still warm, put a fortune across the center of each circle; fold cookie in half over fortune. Fold the half circles over the edge of a large bowl to shape them. Let cookie sheet cool completely before continuing, or use a second cold cookie sheet. Repeat with remaining fortunes and cookie batter.

Makes 12 fortune cookies.

Note: The cookies are pliable only when warm. If cookies cool before folding, rewarm them in the oven so they are flexible. Continue to fold cookies. Do not make these cookies on a humid or rainy day. It will be too hard to fold them and for them to set crisp.

FRANCE

France has always

been famous for its food and its food presentation. The French often say, "The eye eats first."

In France, the first course of a meal is called *hors d'oeuvres* (pronounced or-*durve*), which, in French, means "aside from the main work." This first course teases the taste buds for what is to come next. Some popular *hors d'oeuvres* are a small portion of salad, vegetables tossed with a little oil and fresh herbs, or *ratatouille* (ra-tuh-*too*-ee), a cooked mixture of vegetables. After the *hors d'oeuvres* are eaten, the main course is served. The main course is usually fish, meat, or chicken and vegetables.

Bread is a specialty in France, and it comes in all shapes and sizes—flat, long and thin, round, small, or dark. Some bakers make short loaves especially for children. The most popular type of French bread is called a *baguette* (bag-et), a golden, rod-shaped loaf, about two feet long. Almost all French bread is crusty, and baked fresh every day.

France has eleven different provinces or regions, each known for its food.

Brittany is the home of a French pancake, called a *crêpe*. In Brittany, there are as many *crêpe* shops as there are bakeries. Garlic, strawberries, and apples also grow in Brittany.

Burgundy is known for producing France's best beef, ham, and Dijon mustard.

In Normandy, special mushrooms such as *cèpes* (sep) and *morels* crowd the stores and markets. This area is known for producing the richest cream, milk, and butter. Apple cider also comes from Normandy.

Alsace and Lorraine have a strong German influence because they border Germany. The food from this region—sausages, sauerkraut and cabbage soup—have a German flair.

Bordeaux is best known for its fine wines, its brandy, and its truffles.

The Champagne region is the home of excellent sausages, and champagne grapes. These grapes produce the only wine in the world which can be officially called "champagne."

Touraine is called the "garden of France." France's greatest table grapes grow in Touraine. So do fruits and vegetables, such as cherries and plums.

The province of Ile de France includes the bustling city of Paris. There are many restaurants, markets, and cooking schools in Ile de France.

Franche-Comte is a mountainous province. The cows of this region produce the creamiest milk, which is made into cheese.

Provence, an area in the south of France, is famous for its orange groves.

Languedoc, Foix, and Roussillon are known for their *cassoulets* (ka-soo-lay)—hearty bean stews with chunks of garlicky sausage and pork. This area borders Spain, and there are many Spanish influences found here such as omelets, with peppers, tomatoes, and ham.

You can take your friends to France by cooking up some of its savory food. When you serve, don't forget to say to your guests, "Bon appétit," a French phrase that means, "I wish you a good appetite."

LOOK WHAT'S COOKING IN FRANCE

French Onion Soup · ⚴

This hearty soup has a slice of French bread in the center and is topped with melted Gruyère cheese. You will find Gruyère cheese at the supermarket labeled *Swiss* cheese. The soup makes a delicious lunch all by itself.

2 tablespoons butter or margarine
2 large onions, each cut in half and sliced
1 large garlic clove, crushed
1 teaspoon granulated sugar
1 tablespoon all-purpose flour
4 cups canned beef broth
4 slices French bread
1/4 cup shredded Swiss Gruyère cheese

In large saucepan over low heat, melt butter; add onions, garlic, and sugar. Cook until onions are golden brown, about 30 minutes, stirring occasionally.

Sprinkle onions with flour and cook 2 minutes. Add beef broth; over high heat, heat to boiling. Reduce heat to low; cover and simmer 30 minutes.

Meanwhile, preheat broiler. On large cookie sheet, toast French bread slices until almost golden, about 2 minutes. Sprinkle cheese over each slice of bread. Broil 2 minutes or until cheese is melted. Or you can toast the bread and melt the cheese in a toaster oven.

To serve, carefully ladle soup into four soup bowls; top each with a piece of toasted bread and cheese.

Makes 4 servings.

Ratatouille ·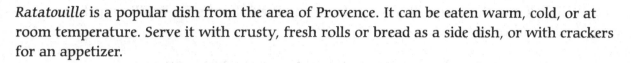

Ratatouille is a popular dish from the area of Provence. It can be eaten warm, cold, or at room temperature. Serve it with crusty, fresh rolls or bread as a side dish, or with crackers for an appetizer.

3 tablespoons olive oil
1 medium-size eggplant, cut into l-inch cubes
1 medium-size onion, halved and sliced
1 medium-size green bell pepper, seeded and chopped
1 medium-size zucchini, chopped
1 large garlic clove, crushed, or 1 teaspoon minced garlic
2 large tomatoes, chopped
1 teaspoon salt
1 teaspoon granulated sugar
1 teaspoon dried basil

In large skillet over medium heat, heat olive oil; add eggplant, onion, green pepper, zucchini, and garlic. Cook about 10 minutes, stirring occasionally.

Add tomatoes, salt, sugar, and basil; cook, covered, until vegetables are tender, about 15 minutes, stirring occasionally. Serve warm, or refrigerate to serve cold later.

Makes 6 accompaniment servings.

Fish en Papillote · ⊓⊓

As the fish bakes in this recipe, it lets off steam and the foil puffs up. *Papillote* (pah-pee-yaute) means "cocoon."

> *4 flounder, cod, haddock, scrod, sole, or whiting fillets,*
> *about 1 pound, thawed if frozen*
> *4 medium-size scallions, cut into 1-inch pieces*
> *1 yellow squash, cut lengthwise in half and sliced*
> *3 small plum tomatoes, chopped*
> *2 tablespoons fresh lemon juice*
> *1 tablespoon chopped fresh parsley*

Preheat oven to 400° F. Cut four pieces of aluminum foil into a 12-inch square. Grease foil. Place one flounder fillet on each piece of foil; top with scallions, squash, tomatoes, lemon juice, parsley, and salt.

Carefully seal packets by folding edges of foil tightly together; place them on baking sheet. Bake 10 minutes. Remove packets from oven and place on serving plates.

Let each person *carefully* slit and peel open a packet at the table. Take care as steam will come out of each packet.

Makes 4 servings.

Quiche Lorraine · ⊓

A *quiche* (keesh) is a pastry tart filled with eggs, cheese, and bacon. The most famous *quiche* is Quiche Lorraine from the northeastern region of France. In other areas of France, the French add vegetables, seafood, or ham to their quiches.

3 strips bacon, diced, see note
2 medium-size scallions, thinly sliced
1 cup coarsely shredded Swiss Gruyère cheese
1 9-inch frozen prepared pie crust, thawed
4 large eggs
2 cups half-and-half or 1 pint light cream
1/2 teaspoon salt

Preheat oven to 350° F. In small skillet over medium heat, cook bacon until crisp, stirring frequently. Using slotted spoon, place bacon on paper towels to drain. Sprinkle bacon, scallions, and cheese into piecrust.

In large bowl beat eggs, half-and-half, and salt until well blended. Carefully pour over cheese mixture in pie crust. Bake 40 minutes, or until a knife inserted in center comes out clean. Cut into wedges to serve.

Makes 6 servings.

Note: The easiest way to dice bacon is to snip with scissors into 1-inch squares.

Salad Niçoise ⬩

This hearty salad comes from the city of Nice on the Mediterranean Sea in the south of France. It makes a great main-course dish for a summer lunch or supper.

Salad:

2 large eggs
4 medium-size red potatoes, cut into quarters
2 cups green beans, trimmed
Lettuce leaves
1 large tomato, sliced
1 9-ounce can tuna, drained and flaked
1/4 cup Niçoise-style olives or other black olives

Dressing:

1/4 cup cider vinegar
1/4 cup olive oil
1 tablespoon country-style Dijon mustard
1/4 teaspoon granulated sugar

In 3-quart saucepan, heat eggs, potatoes, and enough water to cover to boiling. Reduce heat to low; cover and simmer 15 minues. Add green beans; simmer 5 minutes longer, or until beans and potatoes are tender. Drain.

When eggs are cool enough to handle, peel under cold running water. Cut each egg into quarters.

Line large serving platter with lettuce leaves. Arrange eggs, green beans, potatoes, tomato, tuna, and olives in "piles" on lettuce leaves. Cover with plastic wrap and refrigerate until ready to serve.

Prepare dressing: In small bowl combine vinegar, oil, mustard, and sugar until well blended. Pour dressing over salad.

Makes 4 servings.

Potato-Cheese Soufflé ⬩

A *soufflé* is a light, airy mixture made with beaten eggs. *Soufflés* can be savory or sweet, hot or cold. In this recipe, you can use 2 cups leftover mashed potatoes.

4 medium-size baking potatoes, peeled and cut into chunks
3/4 cup milk
1 cup shredded Cheddar or Morbier cheese, see note
1/2 cup shredded Muenster cheese
1 teaspoon salt
3 large eggs, separated, see note

In a medium-size saucepan over high heat, heat potatoes and enough water to cover to boiling. Reduce heat to low; cover and simmer 15 minutes until potatoes are tender. Drain.

In a large bowl, mash potatoes until smooth; add milk, Cheddar cheese, Muenster cheese, salt, and egg yolks; stir well, until mixed.

Preheat oven to 375° F. Grease a 2-quart casserole or soufflé dish. In small bowl with electric mixer at high speed, beat egg whites until stiff. Gently fold the beaten egg whites into the potato mixture. Spoon into soufflé dish. Bake 45 to 50 minutes until puffed and golden. Serve immediately.

Makes 6 servings.

Note: Cheddar cheese is not a traditional French cheese. But unless you have an excellent specialty cheese store in your neighborhood, it is hard to find Morbier cheese. Muenster cheese, which originally came from the Alsace region of France, is available in every supermarket.

The easiest way to separate an egg is to break it into a saucer. Holding your cupped hand over a large bowl, place the egg in it and let the egg white slip through your fingers into the bowl. Place the egg yolk remaining in your hand in a separate bowl.

Bouillabaisse •

Bouillabaisse (bool-ya-base) is a hearty fisherman's stew. It is a famous dish from the port of Marseilles on the Mediterranean Sea. Serve it with a crusty loaf of French bread.

2 tablespoons olive oil
1 large celery stalk, chopped
1 medium-size onion, chopped
1 large garlic clove, crushed
1 28-ounce can crushed tomatoes
1 cup bottled clam juice
1/4 teaspoon salt
1 bay leaf
1 pound bay scallops
1 pound medium shrimp, peeled and deveined
1/2 pound flounder, sole or scrod fillets, cut into bite-size pieces
1 tablespoon chopped fresh parsley.

In large saucepan over medium heat, heat oil; add celery, onion, and garlic. Cook about 5 minutes, stirring occasionally.

Add crushed tomatoes, clam juice, salt, and bay leaf; over high heat, heat to boiling. Reduce heat to low; simmer, uncovered, 10 minutes. Add scallops, shrimp, flounder, and parsley; over high heat, heat to boiling. Reduce heat to low; cover and simmer 10 minutes, stirring occasionally. Remove bay leaf before serving.

Makes 6 servings.

Note: If you don't want to use a mix of scallops, shrimp, and flounder, you can use 2 1/2 pounds of any fish you like as long as it is cut into bite-size pieces.

Sweet Plum Tart ·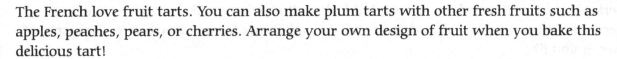

The French love fruit tarts. You can also make plum tarts with other fresh fruits such as apples, peaches, pears, or cherries. Arrange your own design of fruit when you bake this delicious tart!

Crust:

1 1/2 cups all-purpose flour
1/2 cup butter or margarine, softened
1/3 cup granulated sugar

Filling:

1 1/2 pounds fresh purple plums, pitted and sliced,
**   or use 1 1/2 pounds of any of the fruit listed above**
1/2 cup granulated sugar
2 tablespoons all-purpose flour
1 tablespoon grated orange peel

Prepare crust: In medium-size bowl combine flour, butter, and sugar until well blended. With hand, press mixture over bottom and up sides of 9-inch fluted tart pan.

Preheat oven to 375° F. In large bowl toss sliced plums, sugar, flour, and grated orange peel. Arrange plums in a circle inside crust, closely overlapping to cover bottom. Bake 45 minutes until crust is golden, and plums are tender. Remove from oven. Cool on wire rack.

To serve, carefully remove tart from pan. Cut into wedges.

Makes 8 servings.

Raspberry Sorbet · ♨

Sorbet is the French word for sherbet, but it doesn't have any milk in it. *Sorbet* can be served between courses or as a dessert. You can substitute frozen strawberries for raspberries, if you like.

> *2 cups water*
> *1/2 cup granulated sugar*
> *1 10-ounce packege frozen raspberries, thawed*
> *2 tablespoons fresh lemon juice*
> *Thin crisp, store-bought cookies, optional*

In 2-quart saucepan over high heat, heat water and sugar to boiling. Reduce heat to low; simmer 5 minutes. Refrigerate mixture until chilled, about 2 hours.

In blender or food processor, blend raspberries with their liquid and lemon juice until smooth. Stir mixture into cooled sugar mixture. If desired, pour mixture through fine sieve to remove raspberry seeds.

Pour mixture into 9 x 9-inch baking dish. Cover and freeze, stirring occasionally until firm.

To serve, scoop sorbet into individual dessert bowls. You may serve crisp cookies alongside, if you wish.

Makes 6 servings.

Strawberry Crêpes • ∫

Crêpe is the French word for pancake. These deliciously light *crêpes* are filled with a straw-berries-and-cream mixture and rolled. The French spread them with marmalade and butter and eat them for breakfast. *Crêpes* can also be filled with seafood or meat and served for dinner. *Bon Appétit!*

> **Five 9-inch ready-to-use crêpes, about half 4-ounce package**
> **1/3 cup strawberry jam**
> **1 pint fresh strawberries, hulled and sliced, about 2 cups**
> **1 cup heavy cream, whipped until stiff peaks form, see note**
> **Confectioners' sugar**

Spread one crêpe with about 1 tablespoon strawberry jam; top with some sliced strawberries and whipped cream. Roll up crêpes. Repeat with remaining ingredients.

To serve, sprinkle rolled crêpes with confectioners' sugar.

Makes 5 dessert servings.

Note: Whip the heavy cream in a small bowl with a wire whisk until stiff. It will double in volume to measure about 1 cup. Or you may use an electric mixer. While not tradi-tional, it is easier (and safer) to use 1 cup store-bought whipped topping if you prefer.

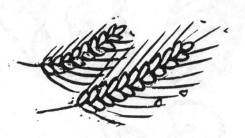

GERMANY

German cooks say

their most important ingredients are patience, love, time, and imagination. They consider these ingredients part of the art of good cooking, and believe that these are essential for making delicious meals that family and friends can enjoy.

Germany has long been known for its hearty food. For thirty years, because of two World Wars, food was very scarce in Germany. German cooking had a reputation for being not only simple and hearty, but heavy.

After World War II, Germany split into two countries—West Germany and East Germany. Food continued to be scarce in East Germany until 1990, when the two countries became one again.

Today, delicious German dishes reflect the prosperity of this united nation. A wide range of wholesome fresh ingredients are cooked in traditional, but lighter, styles.

Bavaria, in the south of Germany, is known for its robust meals. Foods like pork roast, dumplings, or fresh trout are very popular.

West of Bavaria, in Swabia, *spaetzle* (shpet-zel), a type of noodle, is eaten. The Black Forest, in the south, is known for its cherries, mushrooms, apples, plums, and hams. *Sauerbraten*, a marinated pot roast, is popular throughout Germany.

Wursts, which are German sausages, such as *bratwurst*, *bockwurst*, *knackwurst* or *leberwurst* are eaten by Germans in many parts of Germany.

Pigs' knuckles, black bread, sauer-

51 ❖

kraut, asparagus, potatoes, and fresh fruit are also favorites in Germany.

Most Germans have a big breakfast of eggs, cold cuts, and fruit, served with fresh rolls and a soft cheese called *quark*, a cheese similar to ricotta cheese. On Sundays, in the late morning, some people have a second breakfast of cheese, crackers and apple juice.

A weekday midmorning snack, called breadtime, or *brotziet* (brotsight), is usually a piece of sausage on a roll with mustard.

In Germany the biggest meal of the day is eaten at noon. Germans who work outside of their homes eat this meal at work.

It starts with a vegetable soup, fol-lowed by a roast, which is served with potatoes, *spaetzle*, or dumplings. These are followed by salad and vegetables. A light fruit-and-custard-style dessert finishes the meal.

Baked desserts are called *gebäck* (gebeck) in Germany. They are pastries, cakes, cookies, and rolls. These desserts are never served after a meal; they are usually served in the late afternoon.

At this time, coffee shops in Germany are filled with all kinds of people enjoying dessert and coffee—a delightful custom which is called *kaffeetrinken* (cafe-*trin*-ken). This is a special part of the day to meet with friends and to relax in good company. *Kaffeetrinken* is something many Germans look forward to each afternoon.

In the evening, Germans eat a simple supper—a sandwich, a hearty soup or salad, or marinated herring with boiled potatoes.

You can enjoy the best of German goodies by following the recipes that appear on the next page.

LOOK WHAT'S COOKING IN
GERMANY

Cinnamon-Apple Pancakes · ⊤⊤⊤

As a special treat, German children love to make these pancakes for supper. Instead of putting maple syrup on their pancakes, Germans prefer a topping of honey or whipped cream.

1 cup buttermilk baking mix, such as Bisquick
1/4 teaspoon ground cinnamon
1/2 cup milk
1 large egg
1 small apple, such as Golden Delicious, peeled, cored and finely chopped
1 tablespoon butter or margarine

In medium-size bowl combine buttermilk baking mix, and cinnamon; stir in milk, egg, and chopped apple just until mixed.

In 12-inch nonstick skillet or griddle over medium heat, melt butter. Drop 2 tablespoonfuls batter onto skillet for each pancake. Repeat with remaining batter, making a few pancakes at a time. Cook pancakes until tops are bubbly and edges look dry. With wide spatula or pancake turner, turn pancakes; cook 2 minutes longer or until undersides are golden. Repeat until batter is used. You may have to add a little more butter to skillet as more pancakes are made.

Makes 4 servings.

Bavarian Sausage Hot Pot ⋅

This is a hearty supper which is typical in the south of Germany. Serve it with a crusty loaf of Pumpernickel or rye bread.

1 13 3/4-ounce can chicken broth
1 pound kielbasa, cut into 1-inch pieces
2 large carrots, peeled and cut into 1-inch chunks
2 large all-purpose potatoes, peeled and cut into 1-inch chunks
1 small leek, chopped
1 large tomato, chopped
1 cup frozen peas, from 1 9-ounce package
1/2 teaspoon salt
1/4 teaspoon caraway seeds

In 4-quart saucepan combine all ingredients. Over high heat, heat to boiling. Reduce heat to low; cover and simmer 15 to 20 minutes or until vegetables are tender, stirring occasionally.

Makes 4 servings.

Mini Ham and Cheese Sandwiches ⋅

These tiny, open-face sandwiches are easy and fun to make after school. Pop them in the toaster oven.

12 slices pumpernickel or rye party cocktail bread
2 tablespoons honey mustard
1/4 pound thinly sliced Black Forest ham or regular ham
2 plum tomatoes, thinly sliced
1/4 pound thinly sliced Swiss cheese

Spread each piece of bread with 1/2 teaspoon honey mustard. Top with sliced ham, cutting and folding ham to fit; arrange sliced tomatoes, then Swiss cheese on top, cutting and folding cheese to fit.
Preheat broiler. Place bread in large baking pan. Broil 2 to 3 minutes or until cheese is melted. Or toast in toaster oven for 2 minutes.

Makes 4 servings.

Spaetzle • 🍴

The name *spaetzle* means "little sparrow" which is a nice way Germans have of describing these little noodles. Serve them, as the Germans do, instead of potatoes.

2 cups all-purpose flour
1 teaspoon paprika
1/3 cup water
3 large eggs
1/2 teaspoon salt
1 tablespoon butter or margarine, melted

Heat a large pot of salted water to boiling. Meanwhile, in medium-size bowl combine flour, paprika, water, eggs, and salt until smooth.

With a rubber spatula, press mixture through the large round holes of a colander or grater into boiling water. The *spaetzle* will fall through the colander in ribbons about the size of your little finger. Cook about 5 minutes, stirring gently until tender, but firm. Drain well.

Toss spaetzle with melted butter.

Makes 4 servings.

Crispy Potato Pancakes • 🍴

These potato pancakes are crispy on the outside, moist and delicious on the inside. Serve them with chunky applesauce if you like.

2 pounds all-purpose potatoes, peeled
1 large egg, beaten
3 tablespoons all-purpose flour
1/2 teaspoon salt
2 tablespoons butter or margarine

Using a hand grater, coarsely shred potatoes. In large bowl combine grated potatoes, egg, flour, and salt until well mixed. In 12-inch nonstick skillet or griddle, heat butter over medium heat until hot. Spoon 1/4 cupful potato mixture into skillet; using the back of a spoon spread mixture into a 3-inch round. Repeat 3 more times. Cook about 4 minutes. With wide spatula or pancake turner, turn pancakes; cook 4 minutes longer or until golden brown and crisp. Repeat with remaining mixture, adding more butter to skillet, if necessary.

Makes 8 pancakes.

Bratwurst with Sauerkraut and Apples ·

Bratwurst is a German sausage made of pork and veal. This recipe is delicious served with a warm hearty brown bread.

> *1 pound bratwurst sausages*
> *1 tablespoon vegetable oil*
> *1 16-ounce package sauerkraut, drained and rinsed*
> *1 red-skinned apple, such as Red Delicious, Rome Beauty, or Empire,*
>   *cored, thinly sliced, but not peeled*
> *1/2 cup apple juice*
> *1 tablespoon firmly packed light brown sugar*
> *1 tablespoon fresh chopped parsley*

Cut sausages crosswise into 1/2-inch-thick slices. In 12-inch skillet over medium-high heat, in hot oil, cook sausage slices until well browned on both sides, stirring occasionally.

Add sauerkraut, apple slices, apple juice, and brown sugar. Over high heat, heat to boiling. Reduce heat to low; cover and simmer 10 minutes, stirring occasionally.

To serve, stir in chopped parsley.

Makes 4 servings.

Flaky Apple Strudel • 𝄞

Strudel is the German word for "whirlpool." There are many layers of flaky *strudel* dough wrapped around a delicious apple-raisin filling, which is baked until golden and flaky.

3 large cooking apples, such as Granny Smith, peeled and thinly sliced
1/2 cup granulated sugar
1/2 cup raisins
1/2 cup chopped walnuts
1 teaspoon ground cinnamon
3/4 cup finely crushed vanilla wafers
1/2 16-ounce package frozen phyllo (fillo) dough, thawed, about 12 sheets
1/2 cup butter or margarine, melted
Confectioners' sugar

In large bowl combine sliced apples, sugar, raisins, walnuts, cinnamon, and 1/4 cup crushed vanilla wafers. On work surface, place one sheet of phyllo dough. Brush lightly with a little butter; sprinkle with 1 tablespoon crushed vanilla wafers. Repeat, adding layers of remaining phyllo dough, brushing each layer with butter (saving about 2 teaspoons) and sprinkling with crushed wafers.

Preheat oven to 375° F. Grease large cookie sheet. Starting at long side of phyllo, spoon apple mixture to cover half of phyllo rectangle. From apple side, carefully roll up dough to form a log. Place on cookie sheet, with the edge of dough down. Brush with remaining butter. Bake 40 minutes or until golden. Cool on cookie sheet.

To serve, sprinkle apple strudel with confectioners' sugar.

Makes 12 servings.

Note: In America, strudel dough is sold as phyllo or fillo dough. Look for it in the freezer section of your supermarket.

Thumbprint Cookies ⋅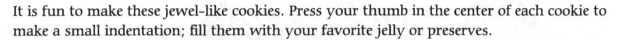

It is fun to make these jewel-like cookies. Press your thumb in the center of each cookie to make a small indentation; fill them with your favorite jelly or preserves.

1 cup all-purpose flour
1/4 cup firmly packed light brown sugar
1/2 cup butter or margarine, softened
1 teaspoon vanilla extract
1 large egg, separated
1 cup finely chopped walnuts
1/4 cup raspberry or strawberry jam

Preheat oven to 350° F. In small bowl combine flour, brown sugar, butter, vanilla, and egg yolk. Using clean hands, knead ingredients until well blended. Shape mixture into 3/4-inch-round balls.

Place chopped walnuts in plate. Place egg white in bowl. Dip each ball into egg white, then roll in chopped walnuts to coat. Place balls on large ungreased cookie sheet, about 1 inch apart. Press your thumb in center of each cookie to make an indentation. Repeat with remaining cookies.

Bake 15 minutes or until golden. Remove to wire racks to cool completely. When cool, fill each cookie with a small amount of raspberry jam.

Makes about 30 cookies.

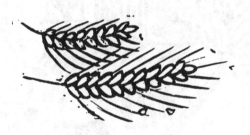

INDIA

India is a large country with many different cultures and foods.

One thing all Indian food has in common is the use of spices, which are important to Indian cooking. The most common spices in India are cumin, coriander, and turmeric.

Some of the most flavorful spices from India are cinnamon, cloves, pepper, saffron, and ginger. Yellow and black mustard seeds, cayenne pepper, and garlic also give Indian food its rich flavor. Curry, a deep yellow powder, is perhaps the best-loved Indian spice.

The word "curry" comes from the Indian word *kahri*, which means spice sauce. Curry powder is a blend of turmeric, cardamom, coriander, ginger, cinnamon, nutmeg, and many more spices. You can find curry in jars in the spice section of the supermarket. But if you lived in India, you would make curry powder fresh every day from a combination of up to 20 hand-ground spices and seeds, and vary the blend to suit each dish. When you travel to India you can enjoy these rich, spicy blends firsthand.

Traditionally, Indians prefer to buy all their spices whole and grind them by hand. Indians often combine fresh ground spices into a special blend called *garam masala*. Many cooks have different recipes for *garam masala*, which is a combination of cumin, cardamom, cloves, and cinnamon.

You can make your own *garam masala* by mixing these spices in a small bowl, then funneling the mixture into an empty salt shaker to use with some of your recipes.

INDIA

Tandoori cooking is an Indian specialty. To prepare food *tandoori* style, meats and seafood are marinated in yogurt and herbs. Then the food is cooked in a tandoor oven, a hollow oven made from clay.

To eat your meals the Indian way, sit on the floor on a cushion, placing a tray with many small dishes of individual portions of food in front of you.

Some Indian people don't use forks and spoons when eating in this traditional fashion. They like to eat with their fingers, using pieces of bread to scoop up food. In India the fingers of the right hand are used for eating; the left hand is considered unclean.

In India breakfast is often yogurt, bread, lentils, and tea. Most Indians eat their big meal of the day between 12 and 2 P.M. This meal is usually made up of five or six small dishes instead of one main dish.

And for many Indians, the day ends with a light meal eaten after 8 P.M. Desserts are not part of everyday meals, but are eaten on special occasions.

Sharbats, sweet, brightly-colored drinks, made with sugar and mint, are popular in India. *Lassi*, a creamy, cooling drink made with yogurt, cumin, and salt, is served with spicy foods. Chutney, a mixture of cooked vegetables or fruits, is a standard accompaniment to Indian meals. Chutney can be sweet, sour, or spicy hot.

With the simple recipes that follow you can create an Indian meal. If you make a meal for your friends or family, greet them by saying *namaste* (nah-mus-tay), which means "hello," "welcome," or "how are you."

LOOK WHAT'S COOKING IN
INDIA

Calcutta Cauliflower Soup • ♫

Turmeric makes this hearty and delicious soup yellow. Turmeric is used as a natural dye in India. Serve Cauliflower Soup with Indian Pillow Bread, see recipe on page 75. Or you may serve the soup with warm pita bread, which is a little like Indian breads.

> *2 tablespoons vegetable oil*
> *2 all-purpose potatoes, peeled and diced*
> *2 medium-size onions, diced*
> *1 small head cauliflower, chopped, about 3 cups*
> *2 garlic cloves, crushed, or 1 teaspoon minced garlic*
> *1 teaspoon salt*
> *1/2 teaspoon ground cumin*
> *1/4 teaspoon ground turmeric*
> *2 13 3/4-ounce cans chicken broth*
> *1/2 cup milk*

In 5-quart saucepan over medium heat, heat oil; add diced potatoes and onions 5 minutes. Add cauliflower, garlic, salt, cumin, and turmeric; cook 5 minutes longer, stirring occasionally.

Add chicken broth; over high heat, heat to boiling. Reduce heat to low; cover and simmer 20 minutes or until vegetables are tender, stirring occasionally. Let mixture cool 10 minutes.

In food processor or blender, carefully puree vegetable mixture, in small batches until smooth. Return soup to saucepan. Add milk; heat through.

Makes 6 servings.

Indian Pillow Bread •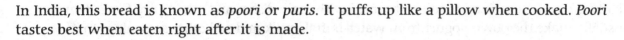

In India, this bread is known as *poori* or *puris*. It puffs up like a pillow when cooked. *Poori* tastes best when eaten right after it is made.

> *1/2 cup whole-wheat flour*
> *1/2 cup all-purpose flour*
> *1/4 cup water*
> *1/2 teaspoon salt*
> *Vegetable oil for frying*

In medium bowl stir whole-wheat flour, all-purpose flour, water, and salt until mixture is well blended. With hands, knead dough until it holds together, about 5 minutes. Shape dough into a ball. Divide dough into 10 pieces; roll each piece into a small ball. With rolling pin on lightly floured surface, roll each dough ball into a thin 4-inch circle.

In 12-inch skillet over medium heat, heat 1 inch vegetable oil to 400° F. on deep-fat thermometer. Or heat oil in electric skillet set at 400° F. Carefully drop 3 or 4 circles into hot oil. With back of slotted spoon, hold circles in oil for 20 seconds until they puff up like a pillow. Cook 20 seconds longer until lightly browned. Using slotted spoon, lift on to paper towels to drain. Repeat to use remaining dough. Keep warm at 300° F. until ready to serve.

Makes 10.

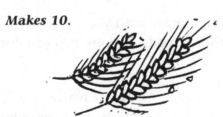

Raita ◆ ∏

Raita is a cool, refreshing condiment served with main dishes and other spicy foods. Indians usually make their own yogurt from water-buffalo milk and add other seasonings to it.

> *1 16-ounce container plain, unflavored yogurt (2 cups)*
> *1 cucumber, peeled and chopped*
> *1 medium-size tomato, chopped*
> *1 medium-size scallion, chopped*
> *1 tablespoon chopped fresh mint or 1 teaspoon dried mint*
> *1 tablespoon fresh lemon juice*
> *1 teaspoon salt*

In large bowl combine yogurt, cucumber, tomato, scallion, mint, lemon juice, and salt until well mixed. Chill 30 minutes or until ready to serve. Serve as an accompaniment to curried or grilled meats.

Makes 6 servings.

Lassi ◆ ∫

Lassi is an Indian drink made with yogurt. Many Indians believe that this is the perfect drink to have with spicy foods. Indians also add finely chopped, mild green chilis to this drink.

> *1 cup ice water*
> *1/2 cup plain, unflavored yogurt*
> *1/2 teaspoon salt*
> *1/2 teaspoon ground cumin*

Place ice water, yogurt, salt, and cumin in a tightly covered jar; shake until well mixed. Serve with a meal or as a midday snack.

Makes 1 1/2 cups.

Yellow Rice with Potato and Chickpeas •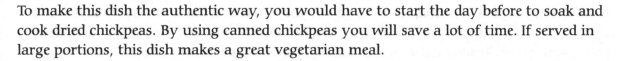

To make this dish the authentic way, you would have to start the day before to soak and cook dried chickpeas. By using canned chickpeas you will save a lot of time. If served in large portions, this dish makes a great vegetarian meal.

> *2 tablespoons vegetable oil*
> *1 medium-size onion, diced*
> *1 medium-size all-purpose potato, diced*
> *2 cups water*
> *1 cup basmati or long-grain rice, see note*
> *1 teaspoon salt*
> *1/2 teaspoon cumin seeds*
> *1/4 teaspoon ground turmeric*
> *1 cup canned chickpeas, rinsed and drained*

In 3-quart saucepan over medium heat, heat oil; add onion and potato. Cook 5 minutes, stirring occasionally. Add water, rice, salt, cumin seeds, and turmeric; over high heat, heat to boiling. Reduce heat to low; cover and simmer 20 minutes, or until rice and potatoes are tender. During last 5 minutes of cooking, stir in chickpeas.

Makes 4 servings.

Note: Basmati rice is a special, toasty-flavored Indian rice. Now, it is also grown in the United States. If you don't find it at the supermarket, use regular, long-grain rice.

Tandoori-Style Chicken •

A *tandoor* is a hollow oven, shaped like a large wine barrel and made of clay. Indians use it for cooking chicken, meat, fish, and baking breads. You can use a broiler or very hot oven for the same result. Traditionally, because most Indians love brightly colored foods, *tandoori*-cooked chicken is painted with red and yellow food coloring. If you wish, you need not do this.

1/4 cup plain, unflavored yogurt
1 tablespoon fresh lemon juice
1 garlic clove, crushed or 1 teaspoon minced garlic
2 teaspoons ground cumin
1 teaspoon curry powder
1 teaspoon salt
1 2 1/2-pound chicken, cut up into 8 pieces or
  1 2 1/2-pound package chicken pieces
2 teaspoons red food coloring, optional
1 teaspoon yellow food coloring, optional

In medium-size bowl combine yogurt, lemon juice, garlic, cumin, curry powder, and salt. Cut 3 small slits in each piece of chicken. Place chicken in large zip-lock bag; add yogurt mixture to cover and coat chicken. Seal bag. Refrigerate at least 2 hours or overnight.

Preheat broiler. If desired, in small bowl, combine red and yellow food coloring; brush over chicken. Place chicken on rack in broiler pan. Broil chicken, 5 to 6 inches from heat source, about 15 minutes, turning once. Or preheat oven to 425° F. Place chicken in large baking pan. Cook 20 minutes, turning once until juices run clear when pierced with a fork.

Makes 4 servings.

New Delhi Kebabs ⋅

These kebabs are shaped like small hamburgers. In India they are a snack food, and are usually spicy. Indians use water-buffalo meat for burgers. These kebabs are delicious when eaten tucked inside a flat Indian bread. Use pita bread for an almost-authentic substitute.

1 pound ground lamb, see note
1/4 cup plain, unflavored yogurt
2 tablespoons fresh chopped cilantro
1 teaspoon ground cumin
1 teaspoon ground coriander
1 teaspoon salt
1/4 teaspoon ground black pepper

In medium-size bowl combine ground meat, yogurt, cilantro, cumin, coriander, salt, and pepper until well blended. Shape 1 heaping tablespoonful meat mixture into a ball. Repeat with remaining meat mixture. Skewer 3 balls onto a 6-inch metal skewer; with hand, flatten balls to 1/2-inch thickness to look like miniature "burgers."

Preheat broiler. Place skewers on rack in broiling pan. Broil kebabs, 4 inches from heat source, 5 to 8 minutes, turning once. Serve with Yellow Rice with Potatoes and Chickpeas, see recipe on page 77.

Makes 4 servings.

Note: In New Delhi, because of the Hindu religion, ground beef is a forbidden meat. You can use ground turkey or chicken, if you wish.

Rice Pudding with Cardamom •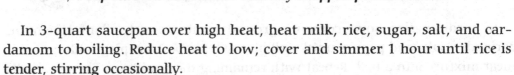

Basmati rice is grown in the foothills of the Himalayan mountains. The toasty-flavored rice and cardamom gives this pudding its special flavor. The Indians use cardamom the way we use vanilla.

1 quart milk (4 cups)
1/2 cup basmati or long-grain rice
1/3 cup granulated sugar
1/4 teaspoon salt
1/8 teaspoon ground cardamom
2 egg yolks
1/4 cup slivered almonds or coarsely chopped pistachio nuts

In 3-quart saucepan over high heat, heat milk, rice, sugar, salt, and cardamom to boiling. Reduce heat to low; cover and simmer 1 hour until rice is tender, stirring occasionally.

In small bowl beat egg yolks with fork; stir in some of the hot rice mixture. Add egg mixture back into saucepan. Over medium heat, heat to simmering point, stirring constantly until mixture is thickened. Do not let mixture boil or eggs will curdle. Remove saucepan from heat; let stand until warm. Pudding may be served now in individual dishes. Or pour mixture into serving bowl; cover with plastic wrap. Refrigerate to chill completely.

To serve, sprinkle top of rice pudding with nuts.

Makes 6 servings.

Mango-Coconut Cheesecake ·

Mango is a very sacred food in India. It is said that Lord Shiva brought the mango tree from heaven for his wife when she found out that it was not on earth. Mangoes, coconut, ginger, limes, and creamy cheese are some of the many ingredients used to make Indian desserts. You can combine them to make this delicious cheesecake—not quite authentic, but still with a special taste of India.

1/2 cup finely crushed gingersnap cookies
4 8-ounce packages cream cheese, at room temperature
1 cup canned cream of coconut, or
   1 cup milk plus 1/2 teaspoon coconut extract
3/4 cup granulated sugar
2 large eggs
2 tablespoons cornstarch
1/2 cup sweetened shredded coconut
2 large ripe mangoes
2 teaspoons grated lime peel

Preheat oven to 350° F. Grease an 8-inch springform pan. Sprinkle bottom of pan with finely crushed gingersnap cookies.

In large bowl with mixer at low speed, beat cream cheese, cream of coconut, sugar, eggs, and cornstarch until smooth and blended. Stir in shredded coconut. Carefully pour into pan.

Bake 1 hour or until toothpick inserted in center comes out clean. Center of cake will not be completely set. Cool in pan on wire rack. Cake will set as it cools. Refrigerate until ready to serve or overnight.

Meanwhile, peel and pit mangoes; cut into 1/2 inch chunks. To serve, carefully loosen cake from side of pan; place on plate. Top with mango chunks; sprinkle with grated lime peel.

Makes 12 servings.

ITALY

Some Italians say

they don't eat to live, but they live to eat!

For most Italians breakfast consists of fresh bread, *pane* (pah-ney), and coffee. Italian children have *biscotti*—sweet crisp cookies—and *caffe latte*, hot milky coffee for breakfast. The largest meal of the day is served at lunchtime. This meal starts with an appetizer, called *antipasto*, such as salami or eggplant. The *antipasto* is usually followed by pasta. Sometimes *risotto*—a creamy, top-of-the-stove rice dish flavored with vegetables—soup, or a dish of cooked cornmeal, called *polenta*, is served instead of pasta.

After the *antipasto* and the pasta course, Italians eat a main course of fish or meat, with a vegetable or potato. Cheese or fruit end the meal.

At day's end, Italians eat a light evening meal. This can be pizza, soup, salad, pasta, or a cold vegetable.

Italy is a peninsula—a body of land with water on three sides—and it is shaped like a boot. There are many differences in foods all over Italy. In the south, the heel and toe of the boot, the sun is very strong. Olive trees, almonds, and tomatoes grow in abundance. In the north near the boot's opening, cream and butter are frequently used in cooking because there are many cows. Seafood is plentiful all over Italy because of the Adriatic and Mediterranean seas that surround it.

The ancient Romans, who lived long ago in the calf of Italy's boot-shaped country, loved olives and grapes, which grew in their region. Olive oil was a big part of their diet.

The ancient Romans had a great passion for food and cooking. And that passion was passed down, over centuries, to the rest of the country.

Today you'll find many types of cooking in Rome. The rich soil of the countryside helps grow great artichokes, lettuce, and beans. In Tuscany, which is north of Rome, there are many Italian specialties such as *prosciutto* (pro-shoot-oh), a salt-cured ham, eels, and dried white beans.

North of Tuscany is Bologna, a city where grapes grow in abundance. It is also where the lunch meat "baloney" comes from, though it is more frequently called *mortadella* in Bologna. In Genoa, the northwestern city where Christopher Columbus was born, seafood dishes are especially popular. *Focaccia* (fo-*kah*-chee-ah), a flat bread,

is also from the northwest region. *Risotto* comes from Milan, which is in northern Italy, and is near the rice-growing region of Italy.

In Venice, a city in northeastern Italy, *polenta* is popular. The region surrounding Venice grows the corn for this famous dish.

Naples, a teeming, bustling port, south of Rome, and on the west coast of the Italian peninsula, is known for pizzas, tomato sauces, and eggplant dishes.

The island of Sicily, which is located in the south, off the toe of Italy's boot, has been influenced by many different cultures. Greeks, Arabs, Germans, Normans and the French have all put their touch on Sicilian cooking. There are many famous desserts and pastries from Sicily including ice cream, *cassata* cakes, and *cannolis*.

To take your tastebuds on an Italian trip, try the recipes in this chapter. And, as they say in Italy, *buon appetito*—eat well!

LOOK WHAT'S COOKING IN
ITALY

Bruschetta ⋅ 🍴

Bruschetta—toasted bread slices topped with garlicky chopped vegetables—is from the Italian word *bruscare* which means "to roast over the coals." Be sure to use ripe tomatoes for the best flavor!

3 large ripe tomatoes
2 small scallions
3 tablespoons olive oil
1 tablespoon red wine vinegar
1 large garlic clove, crushed or 1 teaspoon minced garlic
1 teaspoon dried basil
1/4 teaspoon salt
1 12-inch-long loaf Italian bread

Finely chop tomatoes and scallions. Drain off any juices that come from tomatoes as they are chopped. Place in a medium-size bowl; add olive oil, red wine vinegar, garlic, basil, and salt. Set aside.

Cut bread into 1–inch-thick slices. Toast bread in toaster oven or oven. Place toasted bread on platter. Spoon tomato mixture on bread. Serve immediately.

Makes 4 appetizer servings.

Focaccia ⋅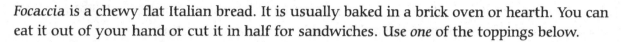

Focaccia is a chewy flat Italian bread. It is usually baked in a brick oven or hearth. You can eat it out of your hand or cut it in half for sandwiches. Use *one* of the toppings below.

1 tablespoon yellow cornmeal
1 16-ounce loaf frozen bread dough, from 48-ounce package thawed
2 tablespoons olive oil
1 large garlic clove, crushed or 1 teaspoon minced garlic
2 teaspoons coarse salt or
   1 teaspoon regular salt

Toppings:

2 tablespoons fresh chopped rosemary or
   1 tablespoon dried rosemary
1/2 cup pitted chopped black or green olives
4 plum tomatoes, sliced

Preheat oven to 425° F. Sprinkle a 15-inch by 10 1/2-inch jelly-roll pan with cornmeal. With floured hands, stretch and flatten dough to fit into pan. Prick dough all over with a fork. Combine olive oil and garlic in small cup; brush over dough. Sprinkle with salt. Top focaccia with one of the following toppings: chopped rosemary, OR chopped olives OR sliced tomatoes.

Bake 25 minutes until focaccia is lightly browned. Remove to wire rack to cool. To serve, cut into squares.

Makes 16 first-course servings.

Polenta ⋅ 🍴

Polenta, a northern Italian staple, is a mush made from cornmeal. Some people in Italy eat it for breakfast. This recipe uses the quick-cooking *polenta* to save time.

> *6 cups water*
> *1 teaspoon salt*
> *1 13-ounce package quick-cooking polenta*
> *1/4 cup grated Parmesan cheese*
> *1 tablespoon butter or margarine*
> *2 tablespoons olive oil*

In large saucepan over high heat, heat water and salt to boiling. Add polenta slowly, stirring constantly. With a wooden spoon, cook, stirring over medium heat about 5 minutes, until the polenta is thick and leaves the side of saucepan. Stir in Parmesan cheese and butter.

Polenta may be eaten immediately.

Or, if you like, spoon polenta into a 13 x 9-inch baking pan. With a spoon, smooth the top. Cover and refrigerate until polenta is set. When set, cut polenta with favorite shaped cookie cutters.

In 12-inch skillet over medium-high heat, heat olive oil. Cook polenta cut-outs, in a few batches, until well browned on both sides, about 5 minutes. Serve topped with additional grated Parmesan cheese, if desired.

Makes 6 side-dish servings.

Neapolitan Pizza • ⫪

Pizza was invented in Naples in the 1700s. It was originally sold on the street. Making pizza is fun. Start with a frozen pizza dough to save time, then choose your favorite topping.

1 tablespoon cornmeal
1 16-ounce round frozen bread dough, from 48-ounce package, thawed
1 cup pizza sauce, from jar or can
1/4 cup fresh shredded basil leaves
1 cup shredded mozzarella cheese

Preheat oven to 425° F. Lightly grease a 12-inch pizza pan; sprinkle with cornmeal. On a well floured surface, press dough out to form 12-inch circle. Place in pizza pan. Spoon pizza sauce over dough, leaving a 1-inch rim from edge; top with basil leaves. Sprinkle with mozzarella cheese.

Bake 20 minutes until crust is golden. Cut into wedges.

Makes 6 servings.

*If you like, you can use the following toppings before adding mozzarella cheese:

<u>Three-Pepper Pizza</u>: Sprinkle pizza with 1/2 cup each chopped red, green, and yellow bell peppers.
<u>Mushroom-Olive Pizza</u>: Sprinkle pizza with 1 cup sliced mushrooms and 1/2 cup pitted sliced black olives.
<u>Three-Cheese Pizza</u>: Sprinkle pizza with 1/2 cup shredded Cheddar cheese and 1/4 cup grated Parmesan cheese.
<u>Ham Pizza</u>: Sprinkle pizza with 1 cup chopped cooked ham.

Easy Lasagna ⋅ ♨

Lasagna is a great crowd-pleaser, and no-boil lasagna noodles make it faster to prepare. You can make it meatless by leaving out the ground beef.

1 pound package ground beef
1/2 teaspoon salt
1 30-ounce jar spaghetti sauce
1 8-ounce box no-boil lasagna noodles
2 15-ounce containers ricotta cheese
3 cups shredded mozzarella cheese
2 tablespoons grated Parmesan cheese

In a 10-inch nonstick skillet over medium-high heat, cook ground beef and salt until meat is well browned on all sides, stirring occasionally, about 10 minutes.

Preheat oven to 350° F. In 13 x 9-inch baking dish spoon in 1 cup sauce to cover bottom. Top with 3 dry lasagna noodles, placing side by side. Cover noodles with additional 1 cup spaghetti sauce, half ground beef, half ricotta cheese, and one-third mozzarella cheese. Repeat layering, 1 cup more sauce, 3 dry lasagna noodles remaining ground beef and ricotta, and one-third more mozzarella cheese. Top with 3 more noodles, 1 cup sauce, remaining mozzarella cheese, and sprinkle with Parmesan cheese.

Cover dish with foil and bake 30 minutes or until mixture is hot and bubbly and cheese is melted.

Makes 8 main-dish servings.

Pasta with Spinach Pesto ⋅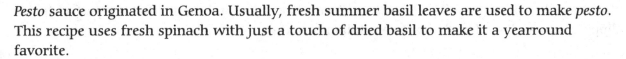

Pesto sauce originated in Genoa. Usually, fresh summer basil leaves are used to make *pesto*. This recipe uses fresh spinach with just a touch of dried basil to make it a yearround favorite.

> **1 bunch fresh spinach leaves, about 1 pound or 1 16 ounce bag spinach**
> **1 cup coarsely broken walnut pieces**
> **1/2 cup grated Parmesan cheese**
> **1/4 cup olive oil**
> **1 tablespoon dried basil**
> **1 large garlic clove or 1 teaspoon minced garlic**
> **1/2 teaspoon salt**
> **1 16-ounce box wagon wheel or other favorite pasta**

Heat a large pot of water to boiling. Meanwhile, wash spinach well and remove stems. You will have about 8 cups. Place spinach leaves in food processor bowl along with walnuts, Parmesan cheese, olive oil, basil, garlic clove, and salt. Blend until ingredients are well mixed and smooth.

When water boils, add pasta to boiling water; over high heat, heat to boiling. Reduce heat to medium; simmer 10 minutes or until pasta is tender, stirring occasionally so that pasta does not stick. Drain.

To serve, toss pasta with spinach pesto.

Makes 6 servings.

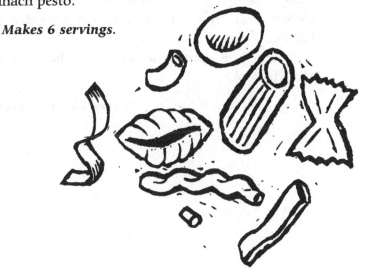

Almond Biscotti Cookies ⋅

Italians call cookies "biscuits." *Biscotti* are twice-baked Italian biscuits that are perfect for dipping into a glass of milk, or for an Italian breakfast.

1 1/2 cups slivered almonds, chopped
1 3/4 cup all-purpose flour
3/4 cup granulated sugar
1/2 teaspoon baking powder
1/4 cup butter or margarine, softened
2 large eggs
1 teaspoon almond extract

Preheat oven to 350° F. Place chopped almonds in a baking pan. Bake 10 minutes or until almonds are lightly toasted, shaking pan occasionally. Set aside to cool.

In large bowl combine flour, sugar, baking powder, butter, eggs, almond extract, and toasted almonds. With fork, stir mixture until combined. With hands, knead mixture until mixture forms a large ball.

Grease large cookie sheet. Shape dough into two 12-inch-long logs, about 2 inches wide on cookie sheet, 2 inches apart. Bake logs 25 minutes until golden brown. Remove from oven. Carefully cut each log into 1/2-inch-thick slices. Using wide spatula or pancake turner, carefully place slices, cut-side down, on cookie sheet. You may have to use an extra cookie sheet, or bake in two batches.

Bake 6 to 8 minutes longer until slices are lightly toasted. Place on wire racks to cool.

Makes about 3 dozen.

Lemon Granita • 🍴

Granita means ice in Italian. This icy, refreshing lemon dessert is served in individual cups made from lemon shells.

4 small plus 2 large lemons
3 cups water
1 cup granulated sugar

Cut 4 small lemons in half crosswise. Using juice squeezer, squeeze lemon juice from lemon halves; pour juice, through strainer, into 2-cup glass measure; set aside. With sharp-edged teaspoon, carefully scoop out remaining pulp from lemon shells. Cut small piece from each narrow end of each shell so they can stand; set aside.

Grate peel from remaining 2 large lemons to measure 2 teaspoons; set aside. Cut large lemons in half; squeeze out juice and add to juice in glass measure, pouring through strainer. Press pulp in strainer so all juice is removed. Lemon juice must measure 1 cup.

In small saucepan over high heat, heat water and sugar to boiling. Reduce heat to low; simmer 5 minutes. Remove from heat; stir in grated lemon peel and lemon juice. Cool mixture; place in 8 x 8-inch baking dish. Carefully place in freezer. Freeze until solid, at least 6 hours.

To serve: Using edge of large spoon, scrape granita from dish. Fill each lemon shell with some of mixture.

Makes 8 servings.

JAPAN

There are some

Japanese people who refer to their cooking as *sappari*. This means clean, light, neat, and sparkling with honesty.

In Japan, cooking and serving food are considered an art. The Japanese believe that their food should be pretty to look at, and that it should taste good too.

Japan is made up of four major islands. The main island is called Honshu. This is home to Tokyo, Osaka, and Kyoto, the major cities. In the north, the island of Hokkaido is famous for its dairy products, salmon, and ramen noodles.

In the south, the island of Kyushu has some of the best seafood, and is known for growing *shiitake* (shee-*tah*-kay) mushrooms. Shikoku is the smallest of the four islands. It is famous for udon—broad, white wheat noodles. There are many noodle factories on Shikoku. People who live on Shikoku eat the noodles three or four times a day.

Rice, tofu, fish, vegetables, seaweed, fruit, eggs, and noodles are popular foods throughout Japan. Fish is important to every meal. And no Japanese meal is complete without small bowls of steamed or boiled sticky rice. The Japanese word for rice, *gohan*, is also the word for food in Japanese.

A Japanese breakfast includes rice, soup, and a side dish which can be fish, eggs, vegetables, or tofu. The Japanese have been eating rice for breakfast for centuries. Breakfast is frequently served with green tea.

Lunch often includes a bowl of noodles, cooked vegetables, and tea.

The evening meal is made up of soup, rice, pickles, and tea, and three other dishes, such as tempura, which are batter-fried vegetables (recipe page 102), ginger pork chops, and steamed fish. This meal may be followed by fruit.

Japanese meals are served on low tables. People remove their shoes and sit on small cushions on the floor.

A *sushi* roll, a Japanese favorite, is like a rolled-up sandwich. But instead of bread, the Japanese use sticky rice as the outside layer. Often, a final covering of toasted seaweed is rolled around the rice layer. The fillings are mostly raw fish pieces, or pickled or plain vegetables.

Specially packed boxes of food are very popular at lunchtime, and also for picnics. The Japanese call them *bento*, which means box. *Bento* is made up of foods packed in attractive containers set inside a larger box. Rice is always included, and can be shaped into rice balls or molded into fancy shapes.

Bento may have a variety of small dishes, such as seafood, meat, vegetables, or pickles.

Portable *bento* are sold in restaurants, on the road, in offices, on highways, or in carryout shops. These boxes are often decorated with beautiful drawings.

The Japanese eat their food with chopsticks. You can buy chopsticks at Japanese specialty stores. Or you can get a pair at a Japanese restaurant, where they often come with instructions on how to use them.

Try your hand at the recipes on the following pages, and use chopsticks to enjoy them. To make your own *bento*, decorate a shoe box, then fill it with the food you've prepared.

On the following pages you'll find recipes for these delicious Japanese goodies.

LOOK WHAT'S COOKING IN
JAPAN

Rolled Sushi •

Sushi are Japanese rice rolls with a filled center. Almost any filling ingredient can be used such as smoked salmon, crabmeat, cooked spinach, carrots, or radishes. In Japan, *sushi* are traditionally served as a main meal dish following a first course of *miso* soup—a light, clear bean broth.

> *2 cups water*
> *1 cup short-grain rice*
> *1/4 cup rice vinegar or*
>   *1/4 cup white vinegar and 2 teaspoons granulated sugar*
> *1 1/2 tablespoons granulated sugar*
> *1 teaspoon salt*
> *6 sheets dried seaweed (nori)*
>
> *Fillings:*
>
> *Thinly sliced cucumber strips*
> *Red bell pepper strips*
> *Avocado strips*
> *Japanese soy sauce (tamari)*

In 2-quart saucepan over high heat, heat water and rice to boiling. Reduce heat to low; cover and simmer 20 minutes or until rice is tender.

Using wooden spatula, stir rice vinegar, sugar, and salt into rice. Stir until well mixed and sugar is dissolved. Cool to room temperature before using.

In 12-inch nonstick skillet over high heat, toast a sheet of nori until it is crisp and fragrant. Place nori, shiny-side down on a clean dish towel. With your fingers, spread 3/4 cup rice over nori to make a thin layer. Make a small indentation down the center of the rice. Arrange some cucumber, red pepper, and avocado strips in indentation.

Lift the edge of the towel and roll nori away from you, tucking it firmly as you go and being careful not to catch the towel in the roll. When rolled, moisten the edge of the nori and press to seal. Place roll seam-side down. With moistened knife, cut into 6 pieces. Repeat with remaining nori, rice, and fillings. Serve with Japanese soy sauce for dipping.

Makes 6 servings.

Japanese Chicken Kebabs ·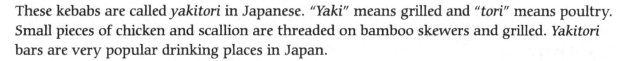

These kebabs are called *yakitori* in Japanese. "*Yaki*" means grilled and "*tori*" means poultry. Small pieces of chicken and scallion are threaded on bamboo skewers and grilled. *Yakitori* bars are very popular drinking places in Japan.

8 6-inch long bamboo skewers
4 chicken thighs, boned, in 1 pound package
3 large scallions
1/2 cup Japanese soy sauce (tamari)
1/4 cup rice wine (sake)
3 tablespoons granulated sugar
Watercress or parsley sprigs

Soak bamboo skewers in cold water for 30 minutes so that they do not burn while cooking. Cut chicken thighs into 1 1/2-inch chunks. Cut scallions into 1 1/2-inch pieces.

Meanwhile, prepare sauce: In 1-quart saucepan combine soy sauce, rice wine, and sugar. Over high heat, heat to boiling, stirring to dissolve sugar. Pour one-half of sauce into small bowl. Save remaining half for dipping later.

Preheat broiler. Drain bamboo skewers from water. Alternately thread chicken chunks and scallion pieces onto bamboo skewers. Broil kebabs 4 to 5 inches from heat source about 3 minutes; brush with half of sauce; cook 2 minutes. Carefully turn kebabs, brushing with sauce; cook 3 to 5 minutes longer or until chicken is tender and no longer pink inside. Serve with reserved sauce for dipping. If you wish, decorate platter with watercress sprigs.

Makes 4 servings.

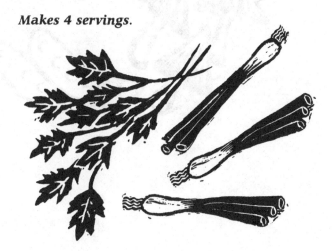

Kyushu Vegetable Rice •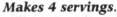

Japanese eat rice with all their meals. The rice is a short-grain, sticky variety. Many homes cook their rice at the beginning of the day in a special electric rice cooker so it is ready to serve at every meal.

4 fresh shiitake mushrooms
2 tablespoons vegetable oil
2 cups chopped napa or green cabbage
2 medium-size scallions, sliced
1 tablespoon finely chopped fresh ginger
3 cups water
3/4 cup short-grain rice
1 teaspoon salt
1 cup fresh or frozen peas, from 9-ounce package

Trim and discard woody stems of mushrooms; slice caps.

In 12-inch skillet over medium heat, heat vegetable oil. Add mushrooms, cabbage, scallions, and ginger; cook 5 minutes, stirring occasionally.

Add water, rice, and salt. Over high heat, heat to boiling. Reduce heat to low; cover and simmer 15 minutes. Stir in peas; cover and simmer 5 minutes longer or until rice is tender.

Makes 4 servings.

Ginger Pork Chops ·

This is a typical Japanese lunch or family dinner. Serve with boiled rice or *miso* soup.

> *2 tablespoons Japanese soy sauce (tamari)*
> *1 tablespoon grated fresh ginger*
> *1 large garlic clove, crushed or 1 teaspoon minced garlic*
> *4 boneless pork center loin chops, about 1/2 inch thick,*
> *   and each weighing about 4 ounces*

In medium-size bowl combine soy sauce, ginger, and garlic; add pork chops. Turn to coat well on both sides. Cover and let stand 20 minutes.

Preheat grill or broiler. Place pork chops on rack of grill or in broiler pan. Cook pork, 4 to 5 inches from heat source, about 10 minutes or until tender, turning once halfway through cooking time.

Makes 4 servings.

Vegetable Tempura · ⬛⬛⬛⬛

The Portuguese missionaries who came to Japan in the sixteenth century introduced their recipe for battered-fried shrimp. The Japanese call this "dipping-in-batter" style of cooking *tempura*, and use it for both vegetables and seafood.

> *1/2 small head broccoli*
> *1/2 small head cauliflower*
> *1 medium-size red bell pepper, seeds, core, and ribs removed*
> *Vegetable oil*
> *1 1/2 cups all-purpose flour*
> *1/2 teaspoon salt*
> *1/4 teaspoon baking soda*
> *1 1/2 cups water*
> *1 large egg*
> *Japanese soy sauce (tamari)*

Thinly slice broccoli and cauliflower. Cut red pepper into 1/4-inch wide strips. In 4-quart saucepan over medium heat, or in deep-fat fryer, heat 1 inch vegetable oil to 375° F.

Meanwhile, in medium-size bowl combine flour, salt, baking soda, water, and egg until smooth. The batter will be thin. Dip some vegetable pieces into batter; carefully place in hot oil. Cook 3 to 5 minutes until golden. Using slotted spoon, place on paper towels to drain. Repeat with remaining vegetables and batter. Serve with soy sauce for dipping.

Makes 6 servings.

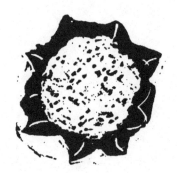

Parent and Child Rice Bowl •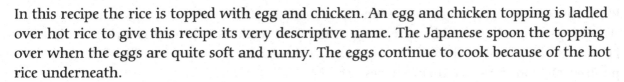

In this recipe the rice is topped with egg and chicken. An egg and chicken topping is ladled over hot rice to give this recipe its very descriptive name. The Japanese spoon the topping over when the eggs are quite soft and runny. The eggs continue to cook because of the hot rice underneath.

2 cups water
1 cup short-grain rice
1/2 teaspoon salt
2 1/2 cups chicken broth
1/3 cup Japanese soy sauce (tamari)
2 tablespoons sugar
3 medium-size scallions, chopped
1 chicken thigh, skinned, boned, and chopped
4 large eggs, lightly beaten

In 2-quart saucepan over high heat, heat water, rice, and salt to boiling. Reduce heat to low; cover and simmer 20 minutes or until rice is tender.

In 10-inch skillet, heat chicken broth, soy sauce, and sugar to boiling. Add scallions and chicken; cook about 4 minutes. Pour eggs into skillet; stir with a fork until eggs are of desired consistency, about 2 minutes.

Place cooked rice in soup bowls; spoon some egg mixture onto rice.

Makes 4 servings.

Fruit Kebabs with Plum Sauce ·

Plum sauce is a sweet and sour condiment made from plums, apricots, sugar, and seasonings. It can be found in a jar in the Asian food section of the supermarket. Fruit kebabs can be served as they are in Japan as a side dish to accompany grilled fish, pork, or poultry. Or you can serve them for dessert.

> *8 6-inch-long wooden skewers*
> *2 large bananas, peeled and cut into 1-inch chunks*
> *1 cup watermelon chunks*
> *1 cup canned whole pitted litchi fruit, drained*
> *1 cup fresh strawberries, hulled*
> *1/2 cup plum sauce*

Soak eight 6-inch-long bamboo skewers in cold water for 30 minutes so they will not burn during cooking.

Preheat broiler or grill. Drain wooden skewers from water. Onto eight 6-inch-long skewers, alternately thread banana chunks, watermelon chunks, litchis, and strawberries. Brush fruit with plum sauce.

Place kebabs on rack in grill or broiler pan. Cook 5 minutes, turning frequently.

Makes 4 servings.

Note: If you wish you can also serve the fruit kebabs without broiling. It is traditional, and also very easy (a utensil rating of 1).

Rice and Bean Paste Balls ‣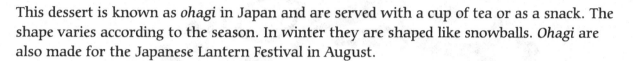

This dessert is known as *ohagi* in Japan and are served with a cup of tea or as a snack. The shape varies according to the season. In winter they are shaped like snowballs. *Ohagi* are also made for the Japanese Lantern Festival in August.

> *2 cups short-grain rice*
> *2 3/4 cups water*
> *1/2 teaspoon salt*
> *1/3 cup rice flour*
> *1/3 cup superfine sugar*
> *1 18-ounce can pureed sweet red bean paste*

Rinse the rice under running cold water. In 2-quart saucepan over high heat, heat rice, water, and salt to boiling. Cover and simmer 15 minutes. Remove from heat; uncover and let stand 30 minutes.

Meanwhile, in small, nonstick skillet over low heat, cook rice flour until evenly brown, about 5 to 7 minutes, stirring occasionally. When cool, toss flour with superfine sugar. Set aside to cool.

With fork or a wooden spoon, mash rice until half crushed. With moistened hands, shape rice into 1-inch balls. Using dry hands, cover each ball in a thin layer of the bean paste. Roll in cooled sugar mixture until coated.

Makes 8 servings.

Note: This dessert may also be made with a center nugget of bean paste and a covering of rice. Roll in sugar mixture to complete recipe.

MEXICO

Mexican cooking is a blend of two cultural expeiences—that of the native Aztec ndian, and the other of the panish who came from Europe o conquer Mexico in the sixeenth century. The Spanish vere amazed by how the Aztecs ooked. Many of their native foods vere unknown to the Spanish. Corn, eans, tomatoes, peanuts, chocolate, nd sugar cane were part of the Aztecs' ood. The Spanish had oranges, limes, ice, beef, pork, garlic, olive oil, and innamon.

The Aztecs and the Spanish wapped ingredients and cooking tyles. Slowly, the two cultures grew ogether and a new kind of cooking vas born.

Mexican cooking differs from region o region. The north, because of an bundance of cattle, enjoys dried beef. n central Mexico, goat meat and

seafood are plentiful. The Yucatan, in the southeast of Mexico, is famous for its tropical fruits and seafood.

Corn is used in cooking all over Mexico.

Tortillas (tor-*tee*-yuhs) are called the "bread of Mexico." *Tortillas* look like flat, thin pancakes. They are made from wheat or corn flour. As an accompaniment, *tortillas* are served piping hot and plain. But they can be folded, shaped, and filled to make many different main dishes. *Tacos*, *tostados*, *quesadillas* (keh-sah-dee-ahs), *burritos*, and *enchiladas*—main dishes made with meat or cheese fillings—all begin with a corn or flour tortilla.

A Mexican breakfast often includes small pastries or sweet bread, called *pandulce* (pan-*dool*-se). Other breakfast choices include fresh fruits such as mangoes or bananas, eggs poached in salsa, refried beans, and foaming hot chocolate. The lunch meal has many courses, which can include rice, tortillas, and fruit.

Merienda is tea time, which begins at six o'clock in the evening. This is a time when people drink hot chocolate and coffee, and eat small cakes. Supper or *sena* is a light meal of soup and a very sweet dessert, which is served later in the evening.

December is a special time of year for children in Mexico. That's when Mexicans break the *piñata* to celebrate the Christmas holiday season. The *piñata* is a plain clay cooking pot filled with candies and small toys. It is covered with tissue paper or streamers and can look like a star, donkey, fish, peacock, or other animal.

Another Mexican celebration, which is on January 6, is All Kings Day or *El Dia de los Santos Reyes*, which is celebrated at the end of the Christmas season.

For this holiday the Kings' Cake is shared by the family. This cake is made in the shape of a crown. It is decorated with confectioners' sugar and candied fruit. The cake is served with chocolates, coffee, or *tamales*—little bundles of dried corn husks filled with cooked cornmeal, which has been sweetened or made spicy with peppers, then steamed.

A small infant doll, which symbolizes the coming of baby Christ, has been baked into the cake. Everyone cuts their own piece of cake. The person who gets the doll is considered the king; he or she picks a queen. The King and Queen have a special dinner on February 2, *Candlemas* Day.

The best of Mexico can be found in the listing of recipes on the next page.

LOOK WHAT'S COOKING IN
MEXICO

Tomato-Pumpkin Seed Salsa ♦ 🎏

This salsa is a fun party snack which can be made ahead. Serve it in a small hollowed-out pumpkin with *tostaditos*, which is the Mexican name for *tortilla* chips.

1 cup hulled raw pumpkin seeds, see note
1 jalepeño chili pepper, seeded and finely chopped
2 large ripe tomatoes, chopped
2 garlic cloves, crushed
1 tablespoon finely chopped onion
3 tablespoons fresh chopped cilantro
Tortilla chips and assorted raw vegetables

In a 10-inch nonstick skillet over medium-low heat, toast the pumpkin seeds, shaking the pan frequently until lightly browned, about 5 to 8 minutes. Remove the pumpkin seeds from skillet and place in a food processor.

In the same skillet over medium heat, heat chilies, tomatoes, garlic, and onion until thick, syrupy, and golden-brown. Place mixture in food processor with pumpkin seeds. Puree mixture until smooth. Stir in cilantro.

Serve with a basket of tortilla chips, raw vegetables, or crackers.

Makes about 1 cup salsa.

Note: You can find pumpkin seeds at well-stocked supermarkets, Latino groceries, or health food stores.

Fiesta Quesadillas ⋅

Queso (keh-so) is the Spanish word for cheese. *Quesadillas* (keh-sah-dee-ahs) are "cheese sandwiches" made with *tortillas*. They can also be filled with many different mixtures including cooked meat or refried beans.

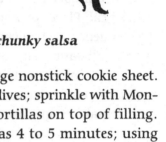

8 6-inch flour tortillas, from 12-ounce package
1 4-ounce can chopped green chilies, drained
1/2 cup pitted black olives, sliced
1 cup shredded Monterey Jack cheese, see note
1/2 cup shredded Cheddar cheese, see note
1 tablespoon olive oil
Mild or hot taco sauce, from jar or can or chunky salsa

Preheat oven to 400° F. Place 4 flour tortillas on large nonstick cookie sheet. Sprinkle tortillas evenly with green chilies and sliced olives; sprinkle with Monterey Jack and Cheddar cheese. Press remaining 4 tortillas on top of filling. Brush each tortilla lightly with olive oil. Bake tortillas 4 to 5 minutes; using wide spatula or pancake turner, turn quesadillas over to other side. Brush tops with remaining oil. Bake 4 to 5 minutes longer, until cheese is melted and tortillas are lightly browned.

Cut each round into 6 wedges. Serve with taco sauce if desired.

Makes 8 servings.

Note: Monterey Jack cheese, from California, is very similar to semi-soft "quesa fresca" Mexican cheese. And Cheddar cheese is a good substitute for tangy firm "quesa blanca."

Grilled Corn with Chilies and Lime ⋅

In Mexico, the fresh smell of roasted corn-on-the-cob is popular on street corners. This is a wonderful dish to make on an outdoor grill in the summer.

4 ears corn with silk and husk
3 tablespoons butter or margarine
1/4 teaspoon chili powder
1 large lime, cut into wedges

Soak unhusked corn in water for 30 minutes. Meanwhile, prepare charcoal or gas grill. Place corn on grill and cook 25 minutes until evenly charred, turning frequently. When cool enough to handle, remove silk and husks.

In small saucepan, melt butter; stir in chili powder. Cook 1 minute. Cut or break corn into 2-inch pieces. Dip corn into butter mixture and squeeze lime wedges on corn. Or you can brush whole ears of cooked corn with butter mixture to make recipe faster and easier, before squeezing on lime juice.

Makes 4 servings.

Chocolate Con Leche ⋅

In Mexico, hot chocolate isn't just a drink for wintry days. Mexicans drink it all year long. To make this delicious Mexican milky hot chocolate, Mexicans use a *molinillo*—a Mexican whisk—or a small hand beater. It is served with a snack such as a slice of sweet bread.

1 4-ounce package sweet cooking chocolate, coarsely grated
4 cups milk
1 cinnamon stick
1/8 teaspoon ground nutmeg
1 large egg

In medium-size saucepan over low heat, melt chocolate in 1 cup milk. Stir in remaining milk, cinnamon stick, and nutmeg; beat in egg until well blended.

Over medium heat, cook until mixture is hot, stirring constantly. Do not boil or mixture will curdle. Reduce heat to low; with a wire whisk or hand beater, beat mixture until foamy.

Makes 4 servings.

Mexican Christmas Salad ·

In Spanish this salad is called *Ensalada de Navidad,* and is traditionally served after midnight mass on Christmas Eve. Toss the salad well to mix; sprinkle with pomegranate seeds for a nice tang.

> *2 large limes*
> *1/3 cup olive oil*
> *2 tablespoons granulated sugar*
> *1 small head romaine lettuce, leaves torn into small pieces*
> *2 carrots, peeled and shredded*
> *1 orange, peeled and sliced*
> *1 ripe banana, peeled and sliced*
> *1 Red Delicious apple, cored and cut into wedges*
> *1/2 small pineapple, peeled, cored, and chopped or*
> * 1 16-ounce can pineapple tidbits, well drained*
> *1 16-ounce can sliced beets, well drained*
> *1/2 cup chopped almonds or peanuts, toasted*
> *1 tablespoon pomegranate seeds, optional, see note*

Grate 1 tablespoon lime peel and squeeze 1/4 cup lime juice from limes. In a small jar combine lime juice and peel, olive oil, and sugar; seal jar and shake well.

On large platter arrange torn lettuce; top with shredded carrot, sliced orange, sliced banana, apple wedges, chopped pineapple, and sliced beets. Sprinkle with nuts and pomegranate seeds if you have them. To serve, pour dressing over salad and toss well.

Makes 6 servings.

Note: Pomegranates are a popular Christmas fruit in Mexico. They are round, with a red-pink leathery skin. Inside are many sweet but tangy pink seeds about the size of a little fingernail.

Fajitas •

Fajita (Fah–hee–tuhs) means "little bundles" in Spanish. Serve fajitas *sizzling hot. Once everything is prepared, let each person get involved and make their own* fajitas.

8 6-inch flour tortillas, from 12-ounce package
1 large tomato
1 large ripe avocado
1/4 cup fresh chopped cilantro
1 tablespoon fresh lemon juice
4 skinless, boneless chicken breast halves
2 teaspoons chili powder
1 teaspoon ground cumin
1 large garlic clove, crushed or 1 teaspoon minced garlic
1 teaspoon salt
2 tablespoons vegetable oil
1 large onion, sliced
1 large green or red bell pepper, cut into thin strips
1/2 cup shredded Cheddar cheese or Montery Jack
1/3 cup sour cream
Mild or hot chunky salsa, from jar or container

Preheat oven to 350° F. Wrap tortillas in foil. Place in oven to warm, about 15 minutes. Cut tomato and avocado into 1/2-inch chunks; place in small bowl; toss with cilantro and lemon juice and chill.

Cut chicken breasts into l/2-inch-wide strips. Place in medium-size bowl; toss with chili powder, cumin, garlic, and salt. In 12-inch skillet over medium heat, in 1 tablespoon hot oil, cook onion and pepper until tender, about 5 minutes. Using slotted spoon, place mixture in bowl.

In same skillet over medium-high heat, cook chicken mixture until chicken is lightly browned and tender, about 5 minutes, stirring frequently. Stir in onions.

To serve, place chicken mixture in medium-size bowl. Set out warm tortillas in napkin-lined basket; arrange chilled tomato mixture, Cheddar cheese, sour cream, and salsa in separate bowls. Spoon some chicken mixture down the center of a tortilla; top with tomato mixture, Cheddar cheese, sour cream, and salsa. Fold sides of tortilla toward center, then roll from bottom end to enclose filling and make a "little bundle."

Makes 4 servings.

Burritos •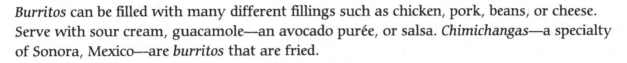

Burritos can be filled with many different fillings such as chicken, pork, beans, or cheese. Serve with sour cream, guacamole—an avocado purée, or salsa. *Chimichangas*—a specialty of Sonora, Mexico—are *burritos* that are fried.

> **Vegetable oil**
> **2 pounds beef stew meat, cut into 1-inch chunks, see note**
> **1 large onion, chopped**
> **2 garlic cloves, crushed**
> **1 cup water**
> **1 teaspoon salt**
> **8 large (8 inch) flour tortillas from 16-ounce package**
> **1 4-ounce can chopped green chilies, drained**
> **1 15 l/2-ounce can refried beans**
> **Mild or hot chunky salsa, from jar or container**

In 3-quart saucepan over medium-high heat, in 1 tablespoon hot oil, cook beef, onion, and garlic until meat is well browned, stirring occasionally. Stir in water and salt; heat to boiling. Reduce heat to low; cover and simmer until meat is tender, about 1 hour, stirring occasionally.

Twenty minutes before meat is ready, preheat oven to 350° F. Wrap tortillas in foil. Place in oven to warm, about 15 minutes.

With two forks, pull meat apart into shreds. Stir in green chilies. Spread about 2 tablespoons refried beans on each warm tortilla; top with l/4 cup beef mixture in a long strip. Fold left and right sides of each tortilla over mixture; then fold both ends under to form a package. Serve with salsa.

Makes 8 servings.

Note: While it is traditional to make burritos with shredded beef, you can use 2 pounds ground beef to replace beef stew meat. Simmer only 10 minutes.

To make burritos into chimichangas: In 12-inch skillet or in deep-fat fryer, heat 1 inch vegetable oil to 375° F. Fry tortilla packages, folded-side down, a few at a time until golden, about 2 minutes, carefully turning once. Remove to paper towels to drain. Serve with salsa.

Almond Sponge Cake ⋅ 🍴

Torta de Cielo translated in Spanish means "Cake of Heaven." It is a light and airy dessert. It is served for weddings and first communion parties.

1 cup blanched sliced almonds
1/2 cup all-purpose flour
6 large eggs, separated, at room temperature
3/4 cup granulated sugar, divided
1 1/2 teaspoons almond extract
Confectioners' sugar
1 cup fresh strawberries

Preheat oven to 350° F. Lightly grease and flour 10-inch springform pan; set aside. In food processor or blender, finely grind almonds. Place in small bowl; stir in flour.

In large bowl with electric mixer at high speed, beat egg whites until soft peaks form. Gradually sprinkle in 1/4 cup sugar, beating at high speed until sugar is completely dissolved. The egg whites should stand in thick, glossy peaks.

In another small bowl with same beaters and electric mixer at high speed, beat egg yolks, remaining 1/2 cup sugar, and almond extract until very thick. With wire whisk, gently fold egg yolk mixture then almond mixture into egg white mixture. Spoon batter into prepared springform pan. Bake 40 minutes until cake is golden.

Invert cake in pan on wire rack. Cool completely. Gently loosen cake from pan and place on plate. Sprinkle with confectioners' sugar. Top with strawberries.

Makes 10 servings.

Celebration Cookies ·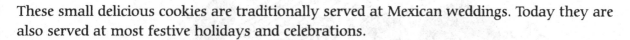

These small delicious cookies are traditionally served at Mexican weddings. Today they are also served at most festive holidays and celebrations.

> *2 cups all-purpose flour*
> *1 cup butter or margarine (2 sticks), at room temperature*
> *1/2 cup confectioners' sugar*
> *1/2 cup finely chopped pecans*
> *Confectioners' sugar*
> *2 teaspoons grated orange peel*
> *1 teaspoon almond extract*

Preheat oven to 325° F. In large bowl combine flour, butter, confectioners' sugar, pecans, orange peel, and almond extract. Using your hands, knead until well mixed and thoroughly blended. Shape dough into 1-inch balls. Place on ungreased cookie sheet. Flatten slightly with bottom of a glass. Bake 20 minutes or until edges are golden brown. Place on a wire rack; while cookies are still warm, dust generously with confectioners' sugar.

Makes 24 cookies.

MIDDLE EAST

The Middle East

s comprised of five areas. There's the Near East, which consists of the countries Turkey and Greece; the Arab region, which is made up of five countries—Lebanon, Jordan, Egypt, Syria, Iraq—and the Arabian Peninsula, known as Saudi Arabia; Iran, a country once known as Persia; North Africa, home to Morocco, Tunisia, Algeria, Libya, and Egypt; and Israel, a state whose population consists of immigrants from about 80 different countries. Because the Middle East is such a blend of cultures and countries, some call it a "melting pot" of cuisine.

Those who live in the Near East eat plenty of cheese and yogurt. Feta cheese is served for breakfast and eaten with bread and olives. Pita bread and rice are popular in the Near East. Cooks from Turkey and Greece use rice in many different ways—with meat, soups, and stews, as well as in dessert dishes. They season their dishes with mint, dill, basil, oregano, garlic, onion, and lemon.

The large meal of the day in Near East countries begins with an appetizer course, called the *meze* (meh-zay) *table*, which is a time when folks gather to converse and enjoy each other's company. *Meze* is the Greek word for appetizer. The *meze* is followed by a main meal of soup, grilled meats, and salad.

Traditionally, cooks from the Arab region cook with spices such as cinnamon, cloves, ginger, and saffron. Wheat and beans grow throughout the Arab region, and are a big part of the Arab region diet.

In Iran, most meals are not complete unless rice and yogurt are served. Rice can accompany meat, or can be mixed with dried fruits and nuts. Yogurt is spooned over rice, soup, meat, fish, and salads; it is drunk mixed with water or soda, and spiced with mint. Yogurt is also used to prepare breads and desserts.

A typical Iranian meal may start with cheese, and cucumbers in yogurt. Then it may be followed with a rice dish, soup or stew, green salad, yogurt, pickles, and bread. The dinner bread of Iranians is called *nan-e lavash* (nahn-eh lah-vash).

North Africa is a place where couscous, a pasta-like grain, abounds. Couscous is served with lamb, chicken, or fish; or it can be mixed with honey, fruit, or nuts and served as a dessert.

Meals in Israel are European in style

but contain Middle Eastern ingredients and flavors. A typical Israeli breakfast is a feast of vegetables, salads, juices, freshly baked bread and rolls, smoked fish, and coffee and tea. At about ten o'clock in the morning, after breakfast, most Israelis pause for a mid-morning snack of fruit and a roll.

Israelis eat lunch, their main meal of the day, in the afternoon. This is made up of an appetizer, soup, a main course, vegetables, grain, and dessert. Later in the day, at about five o'clock, they enjoy a cup of coffee or tea, with a sesame-covered pastry, cake, or fruit tart. Dinner is a light meal of bread, cheese, yogurt, and salad.

Recipes for Middle Eastern favorites are found on the next page.

LOOK WHAT'S COOKING IN
THE
MIDDLE EAST

Roasted Eggplant Dip • ⫿⫿⫿

In the Middle East, the biggest meal of the day starts with a collection of appetizers called *meze*. A large table is set with many small dishes to nibble on such as olives, hummus, and *baba ghanouj* (bah-bah gah-noosh). Sometimes *baba ghanouj* is sprinkled with pommegranate seeds. Serve with crispy *lavash* flatbread or toasted pita triangles.

1 large eggplant, about 2 pounds
2 tablespoons fresh lemon juice
1 tablespoon sesame seed paste (tahini sauce)
1 tablespoon olive oil
1 large garlic clove, crushed or 1 teaspoon minced garlic
1/2 teaspoon salt
1/4 teaspoon ground black pepper
1 tablespoon fresh chopped parsley

Preheat oven to 425° F. Using a fork, pierce the eggplant in many places. Wrap the eggplant in foil and place it in a baking dish. Bake 1 hour or until soft. Carefully unwrap eggplant and let cool. Cut eggplant in half lengthwise and remove flesh. Discard skin, which can be bitter, and seeds.

Place eggplant flesh in food processor or blender along with lemon juice, sesame seed paste, olive oil, garlic, salt, and pepper. Process until mixture is smooth.

Garnish with chopped parsley.

Makes 2 cups.

Stuffed Grape Leaves •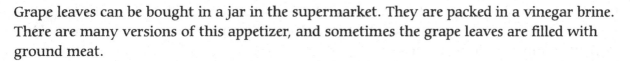

Grape leaves can be bought in a jar in the supermarket. They are packed in a vinegar brine. There are many versions of this appetizer, and sometimes the grape leaves are filled with ground meat.

2 tablespoons olive oil
1 medium-size onion, finely chopped
1/2 cup long-grain rice
1/4 cup pinenuts or walnuts, coarsely chopped
1/4 cup currants or chopped dark raisins
1 tablespoon fresh chopped dill, or 1 teaspoon dried dill
1/2 teaspoon salt
24 preserved grape leaves, rinsed and patted dry

In 10-inch skillet over medium heat, heat oil; add onion. Cook until tender, about 5 minutes, stirring occasionally. Stir in rice, nuts, currants, dill, and salt until well mixed.

Place one grape leaf on work surface; spoon 1 tablespoon rice mixture in center of grape leaf. Turn sides of leaf toward center to cover filling. Roll up, jelly-roll fashion, tucking sides in as you roll. Repeat with remaining grape leaves and mixture. Place stuffed grape leaves, seam-side down in a 10-inch skillet, side-by-side. Place a heat-proof plate on top of grape leaves to weigh down rolls while cooking. Carefully pour in water, stopping when it is about 1 inch from top of skillet.

Over high heat, heat to boiling; reduce heat to low. Cover and simmer 45 minutes, or until rice is tender. Using slotted spoon, drain grape leaves from skillet. Serve warm, or cool to serve cold later.

Makes 24 stuffed grape leaves.

Rice and Lentil Salad · 🍴

Lentils are a staple throughout much of the Middle East. They have long been used as a meat substitute. Lentils are not used fresh, but dried as soon as they are ripe. To eat and be tasty, they must be simmered tender.

2 cups water
1 14 1/2-ounce can vegetable broth
1/2 cup brown lentils
1 cup basmati or long-grain rice
1/2 teaspoon salt
1 large green bell pepper, seeded and chopped
1 large tomato, chopped
1 tablespoon capers, drained
3 tablespoons olive oil
2 tablespoons fresh lemon juice

In 3-quart saucepan over high heat, heat water and vegetable broth to boiling. Add lentils; cover and simmer 25 minutes. Add basmati rice and salt to simmering mixture. Cover and simmer 20 minutes longer or until rice and lentils are tender.

Remove from heat; stir in green pepper, tomato, capers, olive oil, and lemon juice. Toss to mix well. Serve warm, or refrigerate to serve cold later.

Makes 6 servings.

Stuffed Peppers ·

The delicious filling for these stuffed peppers can also be used to stuff tomatoes, onions, eggplant, and cabbage. You can also use ground beef or turkey in place of ground lamb. This is a great recipe to use up leftover rice—you will need 2 cups cooked rice.

3/4 cup long-grain rice
1 1/2 cups cold water
2 tablespoons vegetable oil
1 medium-size onion, chopped
1 garlic clove, crushed or 1 teaspoon minced garlic
1 pound package ground lamb
1 1/4 teaspoons salt
1 8-ounce can tomato sauce
2 tablespoons fresh chopped parsley or 2 teaspoons ground parsley
4 medium-size red, green, or yellow bell peppers

In medium-size saucepan over medium heat, bring rice and water to boiling. Reduce heat to low, cover and simmer until rice is tender and water is absorbed, about 20 minutes.

Meanwhile, in 12-inch skillet over medium heat, heat in hot oil, add onion. Cook 5 minutes. Add garlic; cook 2 minutes longer. Using slotted spoon, place onion mixture in large bowl.

In drippings remaining in skillet over medium-high heat, cook ground lamb and salt until meat is well browned, stirring occasionally. Place in bowl with onion; stir in cooked rice, tomato sauce, and parsley. Toss to mix well.

Preheat oven to 350° F. Cut each pepper lengthwise in half; remove seeds, any fleshy ribs, and stem. Fill each pepper half with some rice mixture. Place filled pepper halves in 13 x 9-inch greased baking dish. Cover with foil; bake 30 minutes. Uncover dish and bake 25 to 30 minutes longer until peppers are tender.

Makes 4 servings.

Greek Spinach Triangles • ⫛

These crispy pastry triangles are called *spanakopita* (span-uh-koh-pih-tuh) in Greece. It is fun to fold them into their little packages. Some cooks make these triangles much larger so they are sandwich-size.

2 tablespoons olive oil
1 medium-size onion, finely chopped
1 10-ounce package frozen chopped spinach, thawed and squeezed dry
1 cup crumbled feta cheese
1/2 cup ricotta cheese
1/2 16-ounce package frozen phyllo (fillo), dough, thawed
(about 12 sheets), see note
1/2 cup butter or margarine, melted

In small saucepan over medium heat, heat oil; add onion. Cook until tender, stirring occasionally. Remove from heat. Stir in spinach, feta cheese, and ricotta cheese until well mixed.

Cut phyllo sheets into lengthwise strips, about 2 inches wide. You will have 36 strips. Cover phyllo with damp paper towels to prevent it from drying out. Place one strip of phyllo on work surface; brush with some melted butter. At the top of strip, place 1 teaspoonful spinach mixture. Fold one corner of strip diagonally over spinach mixture to cover and form a right angle. Keep folding at right angles (as though you were folding a flag) until you finish. Place triangle in jelly-roll pan. Brush with melted butter. Repeat with remaining phyllo dough, spinach, and butter.

Preheat oven to 425° F. Bake triangles 15 minutes or until golden.

Makes 3 dozen.

Note: Phyllo or fillo dough can be found in the freezer section of your supermarket.

Lamb Shish Kebabs ⟩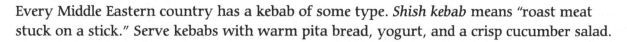

Every Middle Eastern country has a kebab of some type. *Shish kebab* means "roast meat stuck on a stick." Serve kebabs with warm pita bread, yogurt, and a crisp cucumber salad.

> *1 pound package boneless leg of lamb, cut into 1-inch chunks*
> *3 tablespoons olive oil*
> *1 tablespoon fresh lemon juice*
> *1 garlic clove, crushed or 1 teaspoon minced garlic*
> *1 teaspoon rosemary, crumbled*
> *1 teaspoon salt*
> *1 medium-size red onion, cut into wedges*
> *1 medium-size yellow bell pepper, seeded and cut into 1-inch pieces*

In medium-size bowl combine lamb chunks, olive oil, lemon juice, garlic, rosemary, and salt; toss well to combine. Let marinade for 30 minutes, stirring occasionally.

Preheat grill or broiler. On eight 8-inch-long metal skewers, alternately thread lamb chunks, onion, and yellow pepper pieces. Place on grill rack or on broiler pan. Grill or broil kebabs 4 to 5 inches from heat source for 8 to 10 minutes, carefully turning occasionally, brushing with rosemary mixture.

Makes 4 servings.

Sesame Seed Twists · ⑂

The countries of the Middle East use lots of sesame seeds in cooking and baking. During baking, the sesame seeds become lightly toasted, which brings out their full flavor.

1 cup granulated sugar
1 cup butter or margarine, softened
1 tablespoon baking powder
1 teaspoon vanilla extract
1/2 teaspoon salt
2 large eggs
3 cups all-purpose flour
1 egg white, slightly beaten
3 tablespoons sesame seeds

In large bowl combine sugar, butter, baking powder, vanilla, salt, eggs, and 2 cups flour. With electric mixer at low speed, beat until ingredients are blended. With wooden spoon, stir in remaining 1 cup flour until well blended.

Preheat oven to 350° F. On lightly floured surface, pat dough into an 8-inch oblong shape. Divide evenly into 24 pieces. With lightly floured hands, roll one piece of dough into a 6-inch-long rope. Twist rope around your finger to form a coil; place on cookie sheet. Repeat with remaining dough, placing twists about 1 inch apart on cookie sheet. Brush cookies with egg white; sprinkle with sesame seeds. Bake 20 minutes or until cookies are lightly browned. Remove cookies to wire racks to cool.

Makes 24 cookies.

Baklava ·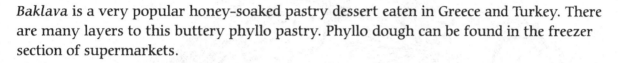

Baklava is a very popular honey-soaked pastry dessert eaten in Greece and Turkey. There are many layers to this buttery phyllo pastry. Phyllo dough can be found in the freezer section of supermarkets.

1 16-ounce package walnuts, finely chopped to make 3 cups
1/2 cup granulated sugar
1 teaspoon ground cinnamon
1 16-ounce package frozen phyllo (fillo) dough, thawed (about 24 sheets)
1 cup butter or margarine, melted
1 1/2 cups honey

Grease 13 x 9-inch baking dish. In large bowl combine walnuts, sugar, and cinnamon until blended. Cut phyllo dough into 13 x 9-inch pieces. In baking dish place 1 sheet of phyllo; brush with some butter. Repeat using 5 more layers of phyllo and brushing with some of melted butter. Sprinkle with 1 cup walnut mixture. Place a sheet of phyllo in baking dish over walnut mixture; brush with butter. Repeat layering, using 5 more sheets of phyllo dough, brushing with butter, and overlapping any broken strips to make rectangles. Sprinkle 1 more cup walnut mixture over phyllo. Repeat layering, using 6 more sheets phyllo dough and brushing each with butter. Sprinkle with remaining walnuts.

Preheat oven to 300° F. On top of last walnut layer, place remaining 6 sheets phyllo dough brushing each with butter. Cut halfway through layers to make 24 pieces. Bake 1 hour and 25 minutes or until top is golden.

Just before baklava finishes cooking, in a small saucepan over low heat, heat honey until warm and runny; do not boil. Remove baklava from oven; place pan on wire rack. Carefully spoon honey over baklava in baking dish. Cool in pan at least 1 hour.

To serve, finish cutting through layers.

Makes 24 servings.

RUSSIA

Russian food

s colorful and flavorful. Russia s actually the name of the argest and most populated republic in a confederation of states once called the Soviet Union. These states, which spread across millions of miles of and, from eastern Europe to the Pacific Ocean, have a rich variety of cuisines.

Over the centuries, many foods and food customs have been brought to Russia from other places. The French brought soups, sauces, and desserts. Germans brought sausages and sauerkraut. Salami, pasta, ice cream, and pastries came from Italians. Scandinavians brought marinated herring. Chinese came to Russia with their teas and steamed dumplings. The Turkish introduced skewered meat, stuffed vegetables, and pilaf. Dutch people brought their spiced honey cakes and vegetable dishes to Russia. These for-eign influences have given Russia a varied and rich cuisine.

Bread is an important part of the Russian diet. Russia has been called the "breadbasket of Europe." In the north, bread is made with rye flour; in the south of Russia it is made with wheat flour.

For centuries, beets have been a part of the Russian diet. Beets are one of the few vegetables that can survive Russia's cold climate. Many Russian dishes are made from beets. The most famous is *borscht* (bor-sht), a beet soup. It is said that there are as many versions of *borscht* as there are grandmothers in Russia.

Salmon, fresh cabbage, sauerkraut, and sour cream are also used often in Russian cooking.

Many areas of Russia are covered with forests, where berries—wild strawberries, lingonberries, gooseberries—red and black currants, nuts, and wild mushrooms grow.

Sunflowers also grow in Russia. Russians press sunflower seeds to make into oil and margarine, or they sprinkle seeds in salads.

Fresh, dried, or canned sour cherries are used in soups, pies, or cooked with roast meats.

Kasha, the name for any coarsely ground grain, comes in many varieties. It is eaten throughout Russia. When cooked, *kasha* is the consistency of porridge. Russians may eat oatmeal *kasha* in the morning, buckwheat *kasha* with dinner, or a millet *kasha* for a late-night supper.

The word for breakfast in the Russian language is *"morning tea."* Most Russians drink tea with milk for breakfast and eat one of the delicious types of Russian breads. Sometimes soft-boiled eggs are added to the breakfast meal.

Russian lunches are very simple and may consist of one or two dishes such as a crusty pie, or fish served with a type of *kasha*.

The first course of a Russian dinner is *zakuski* (zah-*koos*-key)—appetizers. *Zakuski* means "little bites." At a simple family dinner, *zakuski* may consist of sausage slices, pickles, herring, and

cheese. *Zakuski* are often offered to guests, while they are waiting for the main meal. The appetizers can be simple or elaborate, hot or cold.

The main course of a Russian dinner includes meat, poultry, or fish, soup, salad, and a vegetable. It is followed by a rich dessert. An evening snack may consist of cheese, bread, cold meats, or cakes.

Some say Russian food warms the soul. Why not warm the souls of your family and friends by preparing them a Russian meal?

LOOK WHAT'S COOKING IN
RUSSIA

Russian Beet Soup • 🍴

Borscht is the Slavic word for beet. Luscious red beets give this soup its delicious color and flavor. There are many versions with different ingredients, depending on the region of Russia and the time of year it is made.

1/4 cup vegetable oil
1 pound all-purpose potatoes, peeled and diced
4 cups chopped green cabbage
1 large onion, chopped
1 large carrot, peeled and sliced
1 large bunch beets, peeled and coarsely shredded, about 3 1/2 to 4 cups
3 cups water
1 13 3/4-ounce can beef or chicken broth
2 tablespoons apple cider vinegar
2 1/2 teaspoons salt
1 tablespoon chopped fresh dill or 1 teaspoon dried dill
Sour cream, optional

In 5-quart saucepan over medium heat, heat oil; add potatoes, cabbage, onion, and carrot. Cook about 10 minutes, stirring occasionally. Add shredded beets, water, broth, cider vinegar, salt, and dill. Over high heat, heat to boiling. Reduce heat to low; cover and simmer 20 minutes or until vegetables are tender, stirring occasionally.

To serve, top each serving with a spoonful of sour cream, if desired.

Makes 6 servings.

Smetana Mushrooms • ⫙

Smetana is often served in Russia instead of sour cream. *Smetana* is a tangy, slightly acid dairy cream which is a favorite of Russian cooks, and is added to soups, dressings, and sauces.

1/4 cup heavy cream
1/4 cup plain, unflavored yogurt
1/4 cup butter or margarine
1 pound button (small) mushrooms, cleaned
2 scallions, sliced
1/2 teaspoon salt

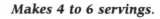

In small bowl combine heavy cream and yogurt until well mixed. This is the *smetana* mixture; set aside.

In 12-inch skillet over medium heat, melt butter. Add mushrooms, scallions, and salt; cook about 10 minutes or until mushrooms are tender, stirring occasionally.

Reduce heat to low; stir in *smetana* mixture. Cook 5 minutes longer, taking care not to boil and stirring frequently.

Makes 4 to 6 servings.

Carrots with Cumin Seeds · ⫙

This dish is usually spicy and is traditionally served with a stew. It is popular in the republic of Uzbekistan, near the Aral sea.

> 2 tablespoons vegetable oil
> 1 medium-size onion, chopped
> 2 cups baby carrots, peeled and left whole
> 1 teaspoon paprika
> 1/2 teaspoon cumin seeds
> 1/2 teaspoon salt
> 1/2 cup water

In 10-inch skillet over medium heat, heat oil; add onion. Cook 5 minutes, stirring occasionally. Add baby carrots, paprika, cumin seeds, and salt; cook 5 minutes, stirring occasionally. Add water; over high heat, heat to boiling. Reduce heat to low; cover and simmer 10 minutes or until carrots are tender, stirring occasionally.

Makes 4 servings.

Creamy Potatoes, Moscow-Style · ⫙

Russian cooks have many different ways of preparing mashed potatoes. Sour cream gives a nice richness to this dish.

> 4 large all-purpose potatoes, peeled and cut into 1-inch cubes
> 1/2 cup milk
> 1 large garlic clove, sliced or 1 teaspoon minced garlic
> 1/2 cup sour cream
> 6 tablespoons butter or margarine
> 1 tablespoon chopped fresh dill or 1 teaspoon dried dill
> 1 teaspoon salt

In 4-quart saucepan over high heat, heat potatoes and enough water to cover to boiling. Reduce heat to low; cover and simmer 15 minutes or until potatoes are tender. Drain well.

Meanwhile, heat milk and garlic just to boiling. Reduce heat to low; simmer, covered, 5 to 10 minutes until garlic is very tender. Remove from heat.

In large bowl, mash potatoes; add milk mixture, sour cream, butter, dill, and salt until well blended.

Makes 6 servings.

Beef Stroganoff ·

Beef Stroganoff is usually made with cubes of beef tenderloin. Ground beef makes it faster, easier, and less expensive. This dish was originally created for Count Stroganoff, Russian royalty. It is traditional to serve it over buttered egg noodles.

> *1 pound package ground beef*
> *2 tablespoons butter or margarine*
> *1/2 pound mushrooms, sliced*
> *1 medium-size onion, chopped*
> *1 teaspoon salt*
> *1/4 cup water*
> *1 cup sour cream*

In 12-inch skillet over medium-high heat, cook ground beef until well browned on all sides, stirring occasionally. Using slotted spoon, place beef in medium-size bowl.

In same skillet over medium heat, melt butter. Cook mushrooms, onion, and salt about 5 minutes until vegetables are tender. Stir in water; heat to boiling. Reduce heat to low.

Stir in sour cream and ground beef; heat until the meat is very hot, taking care not to let the stew boil.

Makes 4 servings.

Chicken Kiev ⋅ 🍴

This tasty dish is named after Kiev, the capital city of the Ukraine republic. The chicken roll-ups are usually fried, but it is easier to cook them in the oven, as we did.

> **3 tablespoons butter or margarine, softened**
> **2 teaspoons fresh lemon juice**
> **1/4 teaspoon dried dill**
> **1/4 teaspoon salt**
> **4 skinless, boneless chicken breast halves,**
> **about 3 ounces each, pounded thin**
> **1 large egg**
> **1/3 cup seasoned dried bread crumbs**

Preheat oven to 425° F. In small bowl combine butter, lemon juice, dill, and salt until well blended. Spread each chicken cutlet with some butter mixture. From short end, roll up, at same time turning long edges of chicken in toward center, secure with a toothpick to close.

Lightly beat egg in bowl. Place bread crumbs in another bowl. Dip rolled chicken in egg, then roll in bread crumbs to cover completely. Place chicken in 12 x 8-inch baking pan. Cook 30 minutes or until chicken is golden and tender.

To serve, carefully remove toothpicks from chicken rolls.

Makes 4 servings.

Apple-Cinnamon Baba ·

Afternoon tea, in Russia, is usually served with *baba*, a ring-shaped cake named for the storybook hero Ali Baba. Traditionally, Russians always eat desserts with a spoon, not a fork.

4 cups all-purpose flour
2 cups granulated sugar
1 1/2 teaspoons ground cinnamon
1 teaspoon baking powder
1 cup vegetable oil
4 large eggs
1/2 cup apple juice
2 teaspoons vanilla extract
4 medium-size apples, such as Granny Smith or Rome Beauty,
  peeled, quartered, cored, and chopped
1 cup chopped walnuts
Confectioners' sugar

Preheat oven to 350° F. Grease 10-inch Bundt pan. In large bowl combine flour, sugar, cinnamon, baking powder, oil, eggs, apple juice, and vanilla. With electric mixer at low speed, beat ingredients until just mixed. Increase speed to medium; beat 2 minutes longer, occasionally scraping bowl with rubber spatula. Stir in chopped apples and walnuts.

Spoon batter into prepared Bundt pan. Bake 1 hour and 15 minutes until toothpick inserted in center comes out clean. Cool in pan on wire rack 10 minutes; invert pan containing cake on to wire rack. Remove pan and let cake cool completely.

To serve, sprinkle top of baba with confectioners' sugar.

Makes 12 servings.

Charlotte Russe ⋅ ∏

Charlotte Russe is a rich, creamy dessert and was created by a Frenchman for the Russian Czar, Alexander I. Our simple recipe is made with an easy French vanilla pudding mix.

1 3-ounce package ladyfingers
3/4 cup heavy cream, whipped to measure 1 1/2 cups
1 3.4 -ounce package instant French vanilla pudding mix
1 cup milk
1/4 teaspoon almond extract
1/2 cup fresh or frozen raspberries, thawed if frozen

Separate each ladyfinger in half to make 2 halves. Line a straight-sided 1-quart bowl, or 1-quart saucepan or mold with plastic wrap. Line bottom and sides of bowl with ladyfinger halves, arranging them to fit.

In medium-size bowl with electric mixer at high speed, beat cream until stiff peaks form. You will now have 1 1/2 cups whipped cream. You may use a wire whip to beat the cream. It will take longer.

In second medium-size bowl combine French vanilla pudding, milk, and almond extract. With wire whisk beat mixture until stiff. Fold in 1 cup whipped cream until smooth. Spoon mixture into bowl with ladyfingers. Top with any remaining ladyfingers to cover. Cover dessert with additional plastic wrap; refrigerate at least 1 hour or until set.

To serve, remove plastic wrap from top of pudding. Carefully turn bowl onto plate; remove plastic wrap from sides. Decorate with remaining 1/2 cup whipped cream and raspberries.

Makes 6 servings.

Strawberries Romanoff ·

This recipe is named for the Romanoffs—the ruling dynasty of Russia from 1613 to 1917. The recipe uses fresh strawberries, each cut in half. You can also use frozen strawberries, thawed if you like.

1 pint fresh strawberries
1/4 cup fresh orange juice
2 teaspoons grated orange peel
1 cup whipped topping, or
  1/2 cup heavy cream, stiffly beaten

Remove the stems from the strawberries. If strawberries are large, cut each in half. In large bowl toss strawberries with orange juice and grated orange peel. Top with whipped topping.

Makes 4 servings.

VIETNAM

Vietnamese food

is an irresistible mix of flavors from many countries. China is on the northern border of Vietnam; Laos and Cambodia are to the west. Across the South China Sea, to the east, are the Philippine Islands. To the west, surrounding the Gulf of Thailand, are Thailand, Malaysia, and Indonesia. All have influenced Vietnamese cooking. And because Vietnam has been conquered over the centuries by many powerful nations—China, Mongolia, France, and Japan—there are also foods and flavors from these countries that have become part of Vietnam's rich and exciting cuisine.

The two countries that have had the most influence on Vietnamese cooking are China and Thailand. From the Chinese, the Vietnamese learned how to use chopsticks and soup bowls, how to stir fry, how to drink tea, how to make spring rolls, and how to cook with bean curd, bean sprouts, egg noodles, and soy sauce. Thailand has given Vietnamese cooking its special seasonings—basil, coriander, ginger, garlic, lemon grass, mint, and fiery hot chili peppers.

North Vietnamese foods—particularly beef and noodle dishes, stews, and soups—are Chinese and Mongolian in origin. Foods from the central region of Vietnam have the reputation of being the spiciest.

Southern Vietnamese cooking is more influenced by Thailand whose cooking, in turn, has been influenced by India. The Thai and Indian influences can be tasted in the curry-seasoned and coconut-flavored dishes, and the very sweet dishes that the southern Vietnamese love.

The newest flavors to be added to Vietnamese cooking come from the French who ruled Vietnam for almost a hundred years, up until 1954. The French lived mainly in Vietnam's three largest cities—Saigon in the south (now called Ho Chi Min City), Hue in the center of the country, and Hanoi in the north.

If you visit these cities today you will still find good French bread, pastries, butter, ice creams, and coffee. You will also see European-style vegetables such as asparagus, artichokes, cauliflowers, and white potatoes in the markets.

Despite borrowing from these many different cultures, Vietnamese cooking has kept its own special character and traditions.

Breakfast is a meal of rice porridge or noodle soup to which chicken, beef, or seafood are added. Sometimes a bowl of sticky rice, flavored with chopped peanuts, sugar, and coconut is served. On the way to work, the Vietnamese often stop by a street vendor to buy steamed wonton-style dumplings or a snack of French bread topped with spicy sausage. Lunch is a light meal, which can be noodle soup or cold noodle salad. Or it can be barbecued meats on a skewer with a bowl of rice and pickled vegetables. At four o'clock, most people buy a snack of tea or coffee and French-style pastries from vendors.

The biggest meal of the day is dinner which includes a soup, fish or meat, cooked vegetables, pickled or fresh vegetables, and salads. Fresh fruit is served for dessert.

Try a taste of Vietnam by following the recipes on the pages that follow. And, as the Vietnamese say—*Chúc qui ban thanh công* (yup we *ban* tahn come)—"Happy Cooking!"

LOOK WHAT'S COOKING IN VIETNAM

Far East Spring Rolls • ⑂

Vietnamese spring rolls are unlike crisp, fried, Chinese spring rolls. Instead, they are rolled in soft thin, translucent wrappers called rice papers. The wrappers are sold in the refrigerator section of supermarkets or Asian grocery markets. The rolls can be made ahead and covered with a wet paper towel until ready to serve.

2 cups fresh or canned bean sprouts, rinsed if canned
1 medium-size carrot, peeled and cut into thin strips
1 small red, green, or yellow bell pepper, cut into thin strips
1 small scallion, chopped
1 tablespoon vegetable oil
1 tablespoon fresh chopped cilantro or mint or 1 teaspoon dried mint
2 teaspoons fresh lime juice
1/4 teaspoon salt
12 rice paper wrappers, about 6 inches round or 6 inches square

In medium-size bowl combine bean sprouts, carrot, pepper, scallion, oil, cilantro, lime juice, and salt; toss well. Let stand 30 minutes for vegetables to soften slightly.

Fill a bowl with warm water. Dip each rice paper round for 15 seconds in warm water until soft. Drain on paper towels.

Spoon 1/4 cupful vegetable mixture onto center of rice paper. Dampen edges of rice paper. Fold the bottom edge over the filling; fold the two opposite edges in to center, so that they overlap filling; working from bottom edge, roll up tightly, jelly-roll fashion, to form spring roll. Repeat with remaining ingredients. Cover and refrigerate until ready to serve.

Makes 12 spring rolls.

Vietnamese Wonton Soup •

Rice paper wonton wrappers can be found in supermarkets or in Asian grocery stores.

1/2 10-ounce package frozen chopped spinach, thawed and squeezed dry
2 cups cooked shrimp, about 1/2 pound, see note
1 tablespoon soy sauce
1 teaspoon chopped fresh ginger
24 rice paper wonton wrappers
4 cups canned chicken broth

In food processor or blender combine spinach, shrimp, soy sauce, and ginger until well blended. Place about 1 teaspoon filling on each wonton wrapper. With water, lightly moisten 2 adjoining edges of wonton. Fold over on the wet edges, forming a triangle. Press out all the air so that there is a good seal on each wonton. Place on waxed paper until all are filled. Do not stack on top of one another.

In 4-quart saucepan over high heat, heat chicken broth to boiling. Add wontons; cook about 10 minutes until they float and look slightly wrinkled.

Makes 6 servings.

Note: Use frozen shrimp, cooking according to package directions before placing in food processor.

Shredded Cabbage Salad ∙ ⫪

Fresh, crunchy vegetable salads are an important part of the Vietnamese diet. Shredded meat is sometimes added to this dish.

> 3 tablespoons fresh lime juice
> 2 teaspoons granulated sugar
> 1/4 teaspoon salt
> 3 cups thinly shredded green cabbage
> 2 medium-size carrots, peeled and grated
> 1 small cucumber, cut in half lengthwise and sliced
> 1/4 cup salted peanuts, chopped
> 1 tablespoon fresh chopped cilantro or parsley

In medium-size bowl stir lime juice, sugar, and salt until sugar is dissolved. Stir in cabbage, carrots, cucumber, peanuts, and coriander until well mixed. Let stand 30 minutes at room temperature before serving to blend flavors.

Makes 6 servings.

Red River Sweet Potatoes ∙ ⫪

Sweet potatoes are a very popular vegetable in Vietnam. In the south of the country, some people eat this dish for breakfast.

> 2 large sweet potatoes
> 2 cups water
> 1/2 cup granulated sugar
> 1/3 cup salted peanuts, chopped

Peel sweet potatoes; cut into 1-inch chunks. In 3-quart saucepan over high heat, heat water and sugar to boiling. Add sweet potato chunks. Reduce heat to low; cover and simmer 12 minutes or until sweet potatoes are tender. Drain well.

To serve, place sweet potato chunks in large bowl; toss with peanuts.

Makes 4 servings.

Shrimp and Vegetable Crêpes •

Crêpes were introduced by the French to Vietnamese cooks. You can use store-bought *crêpes* which come in a package found in the produce section of most supermarkets. This recipe is like a salad rolled up in a *crêpe* and it tastes garden-fresh!

1 cup frozen cooked small shrimp, thawed
1 cup fresh bean sprouts
1/2 cup peeled, de-seeded, chopped cucumber
1 large carrot, peeled and grated
1 tablespoon fresh lime juice
1 tablespoon vegetable oil
1/4 cup fresh mint or coriander sprigs, optional
4 large Boston or Iceberg lettuce leaves
4 9-inch-round prepared crêpes

In large bowl combine shrimp, bean sprouts, cucumber, carrot, lime juice, oil, and mint sprigs; toss to mix well. Place one lettuce leaf on a crêpe; spoon a heaping 1/2 cupful of shrimp mixture lengthwise down the center of each lettuce leaf. Roll up to enclose filling. Repeat with remaining ingredients.

Makes 4 servings.

Saigon Honey-Spiced Chicken ♦

Five-spice powder gives this recipe its special flavor. The spice mixture is equal parts of ground cinnamon, cloves, fennel, star anise, and Szechuan (hot) peppercorns. It is used in many Vietnamese recipes.

1/4 cup honey
1/4 cup soy sauce
1 teaspoon five-spice powder
1 large garlic clove, crushed or 1 teaspoon minced garlic
1 3-pound chicken, cut up into 8 pieces, or
  1 3-pound package cut-up chicken pieces

In large bowl combine honey, soy sauce, five-spice powder, and crushed garlic. Add chicken pieces; toss to coat well. Cover; marinate at least 1 hour, turning occasionally.

Preheat oven to 375° F. Using slotted spoon, lift chicken pieces from honey mixture; set remaining honey mixture aside. Place chicken in large roasting pan, skin-side down.

Bake 1 hour, turning chicken halfway through cooking and brushing with reserved honey mixture. Cook until chicken is tender.

Makes 4 servings.

Beef Satay with Peanut Sauce ·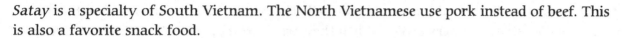

Satay is a specialty of South Vietnam. The North Vietnamese use pork instead of beef. This is also a favorite snack food.

8 6-inch-long wooden skewers
1 pound beef sirloin tip, thinly sliced

Marinade:

2 tablespoons soy sauce
1 tablespoon firmly packed brown sugar
1 tablespoon vegetable oil
1 medium-size garlic clove, crushed or
    1 teaspoon minced garlic
1/4 teaspoon crushed red pepper

Peanut Sauce:

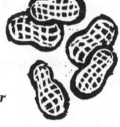

1/4 cup hot water
1/4 cup creamy peanut butter
1 tablespoon fresh lime juice
1 teaspoon firmly packed brown sugar
2 cups shredded Iceberg lettuce

Soak eight 6-inch-long bamboo skewers in cold water for 30 minutes so that they do not burn while cooking. Cut beef into thin slices. In medium-size bowl combine marinade ingredients; add beef, tossing to coat. Cover and marinate 30 minutes.

Prepare peanut sauce: In medium-size bowl, blend hot water and peanut butter. Stir in lime juice and brown sugar until blended.

Preheat grill or broiler. Using slotted spoon, drain beef slices from marinade; set remaining skewers aside. Drain wooden skewers from water. Thread beef strips onto skewers, weaving strips so they form a continuous "ess" like a snake. Grill or broil 4 to 5 inches from heat source about 8 minutes, turning frequently and brushing with remaining marinade. Place skewers on shredded lettuce. Serve satay with peanut sauce.

Makes 4 servings.

Chilled Litchi and Pineapple Cups · ⊓

The *litchi* is a small fruit with a bright red shell. The center is a smooth creamy white flesh with a single seed and is very sweet. When they are dried they are called *litchi* nuts. When you buy canned *litchis*, you will find the shells and seeds have been removed. *Litchis* taste delicious when combined with pineapple and coconut.

> **1 large ripe pineapple**
> **1 15-ounce can whole pitted litchis, drained**
> **1/4 cup shredded, sweetened coconut, toasted if desired, see note**

Using large knife, cut pineapple lengthwise in half (keep leaves on). Using small paring knife, cut out pineapple pulp, leaving a 1/2-inch shell. Remove core and cut pineapple into 1-inch chunks. Repeat with remaining pineapple half.

Cut each litchi in half. Toss pineapple chunks, litchis, and coconut together. Spoon into pineapple shells, mounding fruit slightly.

Makes 4 to 6 servings.

Note: To toast coconut, spread evenly on a baking sheet. Bake at 325° for 10 minutes until golden.

Hanoi-Style Bananas ·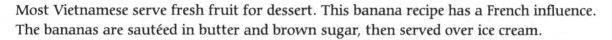

Most Vietnamese serve fresh fruit for dessert. This banana recipe has a French influence. The bananas are sautéed in butter and brown sugar, then served over ice cream.

2 medium-size bananas
2 tablespoons butter or margarine
2 tablespoons firmly packed light or dark brown sugar
4 scoops coconut ice cream or tropical fruit sorbet

Peel bananas; cut each banana into 1/2-inch-thick slices. In 12-inch skillet over medium heat, melt butter; stir in brown sugar until smooth. Add banana slices in a single layer. Cook about 2 minutes until banana slices are lightly browned, turning once.

Place ice cream or sorbet scoops into dessert dishes; top with warm banana mixture.

Makes 4 servings.

RECIPE INDEX

RATING INDEX

Four Utensils

Printed in the United States
By Bookmasters